Remembering

Remembering

A Pastor's Bridge to Spirituality Beyond the Church

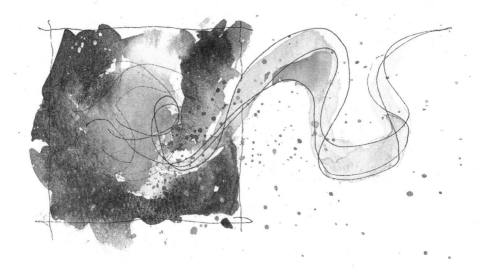

Tim Tengblad

Foreword by Echo Bodine
Illustrations by William Beaupre

Pen & Publish
Saint Louis, Missouri

Published by Pen & Publish, LLC, USA

www.PenandPublish.com
info@PenandPublish.com

Saint Louis, Missouri
(314) 827-6567

Print ISBN: 978-1-956897-53-1
ebook ISBN: 978-1-956897-54-8
Library of Congress Control Number: 2024945679

Cover and interior illustrations by William Beaupre (william-beaupre.com)

To those who help us remember

Contents

Foreword
by Echo Bodine

OVER TEN YEARS AGO AT my Center for Intuitive/Spiritual Development, I was in the kitchen putting out more food for our guests when a very tall, nice-looking gentleman walked toward me with a gentle smile and extended his hand. He introduced himself as Tim Tengblad, a Lutheran pastor. He said he had read some of my books and wanted to learn more about spirituality so that he could bring it to his congregation. I was speechless for a second while I gathered my wits about me. A Lutheran pastor? Here at my teaching Center? He wants what? My head was spinning with questions. Is he serious about wanting to talk with a psychic? Is this a joke?

He didn't look like he was joking. He looked quite authentic. I have no idea what I said in response, I was so nervous. This was the second time in my life that a Lutheran pastor had approached me about spirituality, and that earlier relationship had turned out to be wonderful, so I told myself to relax. He asked if we could meet for coffee, and I said, "Of course," even though the thought of it scared the heck out of me. I walked around in a daze for the rest of the day. I knew something important was happening here, and I couldn't imagine what it could be.

About a week later we had our first coffee date, and I was on pins and needles. I was raised to revere the clergy. I was taught that they are honorable men who are close to God and we need to be respectful of their station in life. In a way, I felt like I was tripping over myself for fear of saying something wrong or being inappropriate in some way. (There had to be some old beliefs inside, because I'm not usually inappropriate with people.) I definitely needed him to take the lead because I didn't know how to start the conversation with a pastor. One by one, all these misconceptions were addressed, and I started to think of him as a person rather than as God's first sergeant. A psychic and a pastor having coffee seemed like a very odd twosome to me, but I soon found out it was exactly what both of us needed.

We began meeting every couple of weeks, and gradually I brought up different topics. Reincarnation was a big one that Tim was interested in. He was also interested in healing, different levels of our souls, and life after death. Before I knew it, we were chatting like two very old souls catching up with each other. We jumped from topic to topic, each so excited to hear what the other believed. I met his spirit guides and started channeling information to him. We had so much fun sharing our thoughts and beliefs.

I think it was on our third coffee date that Jesus appeared to me and asked if I would give Tim a message for him. Jesus channeled such a wonderful message to him, and it left both of us in awe of what we had learned about ourselves that day.

Tim and I have continued to meet occasionally over the last several years, and it's been incredibly healing and inspiring for both of us. He's been a great source of information for me regarding Christianity and the Bible, and I've been a source of information for him about spiritual matters.

I'm delighted that Tim is now sending this wonderful book out into the world. He writes about the truth he has come to know, the truth that he has remembered (as you will see). His approach to this shift in perspective is calm, friendly, open, funny, and loving—despite the intensity of the subject. That's the Tim I have come to know and love.

Preface

ARE YOU AWARE OF SOMETHING within you that knows there is more—more than what the Christian religion has told you? Maybe like me, you're not sure what that "more" is or even what the "inner knowing" is. Are you aware of something within you that is not being filled?

Did you grow up in the Church, but now it all feels a bit "off"? It just isn't working for you anymore—or maybe it never did—but you still want a spiritual foundation to stand on and live your life from.

Do you have a sense that the Church doesn't fit for you but don't know where else to turn at this point in your journey?

Did you grow up in a strict Evangelical, Catholic, or Protestant church that left you with a feeling of guilt or being alone, particularly as you think about leaving that church?

Have you felt like you can't find a place in your church for the real you—the authentic human being that you are? Maybe you have a sense that the real you has to be left at the door, because the Church doesn't do "authentic" very well.

Do you need to hear that it is good to be human and that everything in your life has its place in the growth that your soul came here seeking?

Do a Church's claims that it offers the only "right" way conflict with a broader, more inclusive spirituality that your soul seems to know?

As the surveys say, if you have answered "yes" to one or more of these questions, this book is written for you. You will find a welcoming place within these pages.

I grew up in a family that was devoted to the Church, and the Church became my second family. The members of my Church family had their season tickets, sitting in the same section of the same pew every Sunday.

There was Geneva Carlson, who was so sweet and sat in the pew in front of us to our right. Every Sunday her husband, Joe, would walk up and down the aisle looking for Geneva. "For God's sake, Joe," I'd say to myself, "she sits in the same place every Sunday!" Then there was Erling Lindstrom, who lived on our block. He sang "O Holy Night" every Christmas Eve. He sat two pews ahead of us to our left and always fell asleep halfway through the sermon. I'd watch for it every Sunday and think, "There he goes!" There was Marge Moreland, who taught us the order of the books of the Bible in a song at Vacation Bible School. I can still sing that song today! My favorite Sunday School teacher was Mr. Swanson, from whom I felt nothing but love—love for me and love for God.

The Church family, along with my parents, raised me and gave me a spiritual foundation I am deeply grateful for. They are all gone now, but I smile when I remember them as they continue to live in my heart.

I brought their memory with me when I enrolled at Luther Theological Seminary in St. Paul, Minnesota. After college, I took a four-year, Masters-level program of theological and biblical study, which I managed to cram into seven years. That just shows what you can accomplish if you stay focused!

After ordination in 1982, I went on to serve three Lutheran (ELCA) congregations, one in Ohio and two in Minnesota, for a total of thirty-five years. The churches were very similar to the one I grew up in. They had different casts of characters, but everyone had season tickets.

I had the privilege of continuing to meet and serve so many incredible, lovely people as their pastor. My wife, Doree, and I raised our two daughters, Sonja and Sarah, during those years. I was able to work with amazing staff people.

I loved being a pastor. I loved being with people in their most significant moments of joy and pain. I loved the feeling of making a difference in their lives. I loved giving them hope and comfort and helping them laugh. I loved loving our community and the world with them. I loved how we, together, could accomplish so much more in the world than we ever could separately. A thousand times over, I saw the good that the Church can bring into the world. I owe the Church a great deal.

But then at age fifty-nine, I became aware of an inner voice. I started to remember.

A Pastor and a Psychic Walk into a Coffee Shop

I heard a clear direction from the inner voice when I was on a walk in Boston with our daughter Sonja. In the corner of a store window, I saw a little sign that said "Psychic," and the inner voice said, "Go." Up to this point I had done everything my inner voice was urging me to do, and every time it led me to something wonderful. But a psychic? You want me, a Lutheran pastor, to go see a psychic? I didn't personally know any psychics. Suffice it to say they were never talked about in seminary or in the Church.

But one came to mind—Echo Bodine. I had heard her on the radio and had seen her on television. I had to quietly admit (Lutheran pastors do a lot of things quietly) that she always felt solid, grounded, and trustworthy to me. I also felt this surprising pull toward her that I could not explain. So I read a couple of her books and went to her Center in Minneapolis. I introduced myself to her as a Lutheran pastor. I told her I had read her books and loved them very much. I then asked her if she would have coffee with me, because I had a million questions.

When I picked her up off the floor in her amazement that a Lutheran pastor would want to meet, we did. We met for coffee—again and again. We ended up meeting for two-hour conversations, every two weeks, for a year.

I asked her so many questions. She taught me about the soul, something mentioned but never really talked about in the Church. She told me about the other side (after death) and her communication with it. I began to see this life from the perspective of the other side, which was so helpful. She told me about spirit guides and angels. She told me about our soul's prebirth planning. Then came visits—first from her angel, Lilli, and then from Jesus. Echo also had questions for me about the Bible and the Church world that I came from.

Ah yes, we were just your typical psychic and Lutheran pastor chatting over coffee on a regular basis! There we were in a coffee shop, with all of that going on. We probably spent more time laughing than anything else. I'd look around at other people and think, "If you only knew what is happening at *this* table!" But even there, none of it felt unfamiliar to my soul. It felt like she was helping me remember Home.

So a friendship developed that continues to this day. I am so deeply grateful for her, for that little sign in a window in Boston, and for my inner voice's "Go!"

I opened myself up to many other experiences that I *thought* were new to me. And through it all, I began to remember ...

Introduction

THIS BOOK IS WRITTEN TO help us remember what we truly are. Given our humanity, remembering is a challenge we are given, one our souls have chosen to take on. What we remember is something we have, of course, already experienced. Something reminds us, and what we already know rises back up into our consciousness.

I have come to understand that what is called spiritual "enlightenment" or "awakening" is actually a remembering. It is a rising up into our consciousness of what the soul already knows, at some level. It is like waking up and having a vague memory of a dream whose bits and pieces remain in our consciousness but can't be remembered in full.

This rising up, while often pleasant, may not always be so. It has sometimes caused sadness and frustration within me, as I've grown increasingly aware of the great disconnection between the following messages of the Church and of my inner knowing.

1. *God is a Being.*

    I affirm that God is Oneness. God is within everything, and everything is in God.

2. *God is separate from you, and you are separate from God.*

    I affirm that nothing is separate from God. Separation is impossible.

3. *You are a sinner by nature.*

    I affirm that we do harmful things to ourselves and others because we have forgotten our true nature, which is Love.

4. *You need God to forgive you.*

    I affirm that the idea of forgiveness implies judgment, but in fact God is Love, and Love has no interest in or need for judgment.

15

5. *Jesus died on a cross so God can forgive and accept you.*

I affirm that Love would never require such a horrendous act in order to love and accept you.

6. *Getting into heaven is the primary goal of life on earth.*

I affirm that the primary goals of life on earth center around the soul's growth and development. In fact, every soul makes the journey back into the Love from which it came, after the death of the body.

7. *Salvation means being forgiven by God so that your individual soul can get into heaven when you die.*

I affirm that God is the One energy that lives within everyone. Consequently, salvation is about letting go of our small self and finding our true self in the Whole.

8. *Your humanity is something to be ashamed of.*

I affirm that our humanity is a gift and serves a vital purpose in helping us grow into our natural divinity.

9. *God is there to help you have the life you want and to keep away what you don't want.*

I affirm that many of our joys and our challenges are all part of the lives our souls choose before incarnating and during our time on Earth. Both are our teachers in this Earth School for the soul.

10. *Jesus intended to start a religion.*

I affirm that doing so would have contradicted the Oneness that he taught and lived.

Do you feel your own disconnect as you read these statements? The reason is that you have a treasure within you, the treasure that you came here with. This treasure is the truth that You Are Love.

Jesus spoke of how valuable this treasure is:

> *"The Kingdom is like a treasure a man found hidden in a field.*
> *And when he found it, he hid it again, and went and sold all he*
> *had so he could buy that field." —Matthew 13:44*

That truth that You Are Love has been hidden from you, buried by what you have *not* been told, and buried by what you *have* been told. For example, you have not been told that you *can know spiritual things*—not merely believe in them or hope that they are true. This knowing is not a matter of pride or ego. It is a humble knowing—humbled by our inability to put it into words—and yet we know.

I grew up in the Church in the 1950s and 1960s, which were the last years of the heyday of Church attendance in the United States. I reflected on how the Church has lost its prominent place in people's lives and wrote the following:

> *They came.*
> *They came in great numbers.*
> *They came with their treasure.*
> *How could they not? They were their treasure.*
> *But no one spoke of their treasure to them.*
> *And so they left, taking their treasure with them.*
> *For something seemed to be missing. Off.*
> *Was it a forgetting that led them to leave,*
> *or rather a remembering?*
> *For treasures keep speaking until they are found.*

Some have told me that they feel cheated after reading this book, because the Church did not help them remember the treasure that their soul brought along when it incarnated here on earth. Instead the Church went in the opposite direction and told them that their very nature was the problem. It buried their treasure, too often covering it with guilt and shame.

Why did the Church and its leaders not tell you the truth about your treasure? Because no one told them! And no one told them because no one told those who could have been truth-tellers before them. If they had been told, they would have shouted it from the mountaintops, because the truth that You Are Love is the greatest and most precious treasure.

―――――――

Note: This book is the telling of my story in the context of thirteen fictional conversations I have with "Sam" over the course of a summer.

Part 1

1
At Ole's Tavern: Being Human

"IT'S AMAZING WHERE LIFE CAN take you," I thought, "if you're willing to be led to where you've always been."

There I was, in the parking lot at Ole's Tavern, waiting for Sam. I met Sam at a workshop I was leading one summer. He had joined a circle of seekers, who were driven by something within. Sam was surprised by much of what I said at the workshop, especially that the message of Jesus is "to know and live from our natural Oneness with God, with everyone, and with everything." He had not expected to hear such a thing from a retired Lutheran pastor.

During a break, Sam told me that he had grown up in the Church, but he hadn't heard anything about "Oneness" there. He wondered how a pastor could arrive at such an idea. He wondered about something else.

"I'm not feeling much Oneness in my life these days," Sam said. "But something in me was drawn toward what you were saying."

"Sam, that's what spiritual teachers do. They don't give you anything you don't already have. They just put words to what has always been within you. Those words come in, touch what is already there, and cause it to rise up into your awareness."

"I want to know more about what's already there," Sam said, pointing to his heart. "Would you be willing to meet with me sometime?"

"Sure. How about Ole's Tavern? It's a long-time favorite of mine."

On that early-summer day I saw the familiar cars in the parking lot, and I knew that many of the regulars were there.

"Perfect attendance," I assured myself. "They can help Sam remember."

Sam arrived and we walked in together. Sue saw me from the bar. "Tim! Good to see you. Having the usual?" I gave her a thumbs-up, and she called out, "One Alaskan Amber coming up!"

"This is my friend Sam. Sam, this is the owner, Sue."

"Welcome, my friend. Do you know what you want?"

"I'll have a Sam—Sam Adams."

My usual spot was open, a booth under the old Smoke Eater from days long gone. As we made our way over, I exchanged greetings with a couple of regulars, Margie and Peter, who have season tickets two booths down from mine. I always hope to see them. They clearly love each other deeply, and they treat everyone around them with amazing kindness and gentleness. They help me remember.

Sam said, "What is this place anyway? Your *Cheers*?"

"Ha! Well, Sam, I guess we all like to go where everybody knows our name."

We chatted a bit, and Sue brought our beers over. Nodding toward me, she said to Sam, "Be careful of this one. Don't believe a word he says. He's so full of it!" Sue put her hand on Sam's shoulder. "Welcome, my friend."

As she walked back to the bar, I raised my glass. "They're onto me here, Sam! She is one of the wisest people I've ever known, that Sue. Says she loves her job because she loves studying people. I've learned so much from her. There are some real case studies in this place! She should have her PhD by now.

"Sue and her husband, Tom, owned Ole's Tavern for thirty years. Tom was killed in a car accident two years ago. We had a memorial service for him right here—probably one of the most meaningful services I was ever part of. We mostly shared stories. Since then, this place has pretty much been Sue's life. That's Tom's picture back of the bar. Tom showed a natural respect, a reverence, for everyone. He knew the name of every person who came through that door. If he didn't, he made sure he found out. He made everyone feel welcome, seen, accepted. We all miss him."

As we took our first sips, Sam asked me how often I come here. "I've been meeting an old friend, Joe, here for thirty years. We've known each other since junior high. There's a line from a song by Steve Chapin that I love:

Old friends. They mean much more to me than my new friends.
They can see where you are, and they know where you've been.

"Joe and I have shared a lot. The first thing that brought us to-gether was our both being skinny growing up. That was especially hard in the 1950s and 1960s. Men were supposed to be macho, big, strong, tough guys. But we weren't at all, so we were bullied and laughed at. The girls were bullied for the opposite reason. They were *supposed* to be skinny. So any girl that didn't fit the expectations, well, I knew what they were going through.

"I grew up playing and loving sports, but I couldn't take being laughed at for being skinny. So in junior high, I stopped playing my favorite sport, basketball. It was hard sitting there just watching guys I'd played with."

I looked over at someone at the bar. "It's tough identifying so strongly with these bodies while we're in them. Almost everyone struggles with their body, wishing it was different. Some of us wish *desperately*. One person wants more of this and less of that—another wants less of this and more of that. We get to where we don't even like *ourselves*, as if we are our bodies."

"Tim, even athletes struggle with their bodies."

"Yeah, I'm sure. What impressed me about Joe was that he had the guts to wear shorts in public. That was something I didn't have the courage to do. I was too self-conscious. But Joe—it was hard for him too, but he actually *did* it! And I admired his courage and self-acceptance.

With my eyes settling on my friends, I smiled. "I love coming here, Sam, because they don't treat me like a pastor. You know what I mean? They treat me like a normal human being. I love that, because that is SO what I am. It's good to be human, Sam. Your soul chose it. Being human is good for the soul."

Sam looked puzzled. "I'm having trouble seeing *that* these days."

"I'd love to talk about that sometime. When people find out you're a pastor, they get kind of weird around you. So I like coming here. I'm just a guy at the local watering hole."

Sam came back with, "Yeah, I get that. When I was growing up, our pastor seemed, I don't know, not like a regular guy."

I laughed. "Well, I suppose putting someone in a dress like no one else is wearing, setting them up on stage in a sanctuary, and hearing them talk about God all the time would do that."

"Did you *like* being a pastor?" Sam asked.

I laughed. "Well, the communion-wafer tasting parties were always fun! Yeah, I loved a lot of things about being a pastor. I counted it a privilege to be invited into the most profound moments of people's lives, from the saddest of the sad, to the happiest. I loved loving those people and learning from them."

I noticed Sam gazing off into space. "What are you thinking about, Sam?"

He laughed. "Oh, I was just picturing a communion-wafer tasting party. Anyway, did you always *want* to be a pastor?"

"I was one of those who struggled to find their place in the world. Part of my struggle was that from an early age, around ten or so, I had my parents' friends telling me, 'Oh, you'd be such a good pastor!' Souls don't actually do well being told what they should be and do. They're here to discover that for themselves."

As Sam took a drink, I continued. "A big part of my early life was playing golf with my dad. When I was young, my dad started taking me out to the golf course with him, and I loved it. We had some of our best times together there. It was where we did our best talking. I loved those times. So the golf course became a happy place for me."

Sam shook his head. "Didn't have anything like that with *my* father."

"I'm sorry, Sam."

"It was what it was. Go ahead, Tim. You were talking about golf?"

"It's amazing, Sam, how in looking back you can see how the pieces have fit together. Because I fell in love with the game while playing with my dad, I played high school and college golf. I played tournaments in the summer. That's how I met my wife. I was playing in a tournament in my hometown, and I went out to a bar to listen to her sing. I had met her briefly before. Went back four nights in a row. Fell in love. Two years later, we got married. She's the best thing that ever happened to me. An amazing person. I won the freakin' lottery!"

I showed Sam a picture of my family. "Two daughters, two sons-in-law, and two grandchildren. But enough about me. What do you do for a living?"

"I'm a high school physics teacher. I have two kids—Ben, fifteen, and Avery, thirteen. Avery is special needs, and she has some other health issues.

"I grew up in a pretty dysfunctional family. My mom did her best, but had her stuff. My dad was an alcoholic, and not fun to be around, especially when he drank. My sister and I kind of danced around him. My folks got divorced when I left for college. They didn't have to wait until then. I actually wish they hadn't."

Sam looked over at a couple sitting at the bar. "I was married. We divorced two years ago. Growing up, I was a jock. Football, basketball, and baseball were my refuge. Got a basketball scholarship for college, where I met Jadyn our freshman year. I knew the first time I saw her that I'd marry her. We both thought it was a match made in heaven, and it was—for the early years. We married right out of college. I started teaching. Jadyn began working as a physical therapist."

"Sam, you lived the life I wanted when I was young. Be a jock. Meet the girl. I didn't have a girlfriend in high school or in college. I wanted that so badly, but it never really happened until I was twenty-five and met my wife. There was a time I was worried that I would never get married or have my own family."

I started laughing. "We're so funny when we're human! We get our undies all in a bunch about our stuff, but the Universe has it all covered in its own way—its better way. Turned out 'my love' was an hour away from me the whole time! The timing just needed to be right."

Looking over at the television above the bar, I saw a father talking to his daughter. "Tell me about Avery."

Sam smiled, "Avery is amazing. She has Down syndrome. At first, you go through a kind of grief at losing the life you thought was coming. It *is* very hard at times, but she's taught me so much. Sometimes I wonder who's the one with the challenge—me or her?"

"I love that, Sam! I'd like to hear more about her. And how about Ben?"

"I see so much of me in Ben. He's a jock. Loves basketball and baseball. He's a good kid. I'm proud of them both. I grew up with my parents taking me to church on Sundays. I liked the youth group stuff and the summer mission trips. Good times. The rest of the church stuff, I don't know. Didn't click with me. Guess I just had trouble with organized religion."

"Ha! You should have come to the church where I was the pastor. We were never that organized!"

Sam laughed, and then I asked, "What didn't click?"

"The Sunday morning thing. Our pastor was a nice enough guy but kind of boring. And it was the same thing, over and over. I couldn't see how it related to my life. These days I'd call myself spiritual but not religious."

"What does the word 'spiritual' mean for you, Sam?"

"Connection. Meaning. Purpose. Love. Sense of wellbeing. I believe in an intelligence bigger than me that's driving the bus, you might say. I just have a sense that there's a reason for everything."

"Thanks for that, Sam. There's a lot there."

"Sure, but what made you want to be a part of the *religious* world, as a pastor?"

"Oh my. Deciding to be a pastor. Well, it took me a long time to get there. Growing up, I was kind of like you. My friends were all at church, so that was mostly why I loved being there. I had the idea of being a pastor rolling around in the back of my mind in college, but after graduation, I still wasn't sure. So after college, I took a year off and traveled. During that year I got some advice from a pastor in Chicago that really helped me with a lot of things in life. I was talking with him about my uncertainties about becoming a pastor, and he told me, 'Don't be one, unless you can't *not* be one.' In the toughest times, that advice guided me. Every time I thought about not being a pastor, I just couldn't go there."

I looked over at Sue as she let out her trademark laugh. She was listening to Carl, one of the regulars. Laughter doesn't happen often when you're listening to Carl. The poor guy could make espresso nervous, and he's usually a surefire cure for happiness. But Sue's good for Carl. She steadies him.

"As much as I liked being a pastor and loved the people, there was an ache in my heart that no one knew was there. I felt it, but I never really understood what it was until it was finally gone. I was like you, Sam. Something just seemed, I don't know, 'off' about traditional Christianity. Then when I was fifty-nine—twenty-nine years into my ministry—what I had been searching for came into my awareness. Turns out, it was there all along. I'm happy to talk with you about that, because what's true for me is also true for you. It's true for everyone and everything. I guess that's why we're talking here."

After a couple of sips, Sam looked over at Sue. She was doing her thing again, gently putting her hand on the arm of another regular, Cheryl, embracing her with those tender eyes. Cheryl is a lovely woman, with a fierce love for her kids, one of whom is struggling with chemo treatments.

"Is there anything that you can't *not* do, Sam?"

After looking out the window for a moment, Sam answered, "I can't not love my kids. Hmm. I never really thought about it like that, but the good stuff really is in the things you can't not do."

"We are blessed when we're doing something that we just *have* to do, Sam. Right there is that meaning and purpose you mentioned earlier."

We talked about many things that day, and at one point Sam said, "So at the workshop, I asked you about Jesus trying to help us 'know and live from our Oneness.' How did you get *there*?"

I looked into the back room. "See those two women sitting over there? They're retired judges. They connected through their mutual frustration with seeing the same kids coming through the court system again and again. Kids they knew had potential.

"They created a program called 'Promise.' It's a collaboration between the judicial system and other local agencies. They met a couple of cops here at Ole's Tavern who got law enforcement involved. They hold court here now to plan. I want you to meet them."

We walked over and I stopped near their table. "Permission to approach the bench?"

They both laughed. "Granted."

"Juanita and Aisha, this is my friend Sam." Finding out Sam was a high school teacher, they talked about kids, troubled homes, and Promise.

"You just have to remember," Aisha said, "they're all good at heart. They just need someone to help them see it."

"Awesome," Sam said as we walked back to our table. "You talk to people like that, and you're hopeful."

"Sam, I didn't suggest meeting here to *talk* about Oneness. I suggested Ole's Tavern so you could *experience* Oneness. Know it.

Feel it. Feel what rises up within you. Experience is the teacher that transforms."

After sitting down, I looked at Sam. "Remember what I said at the workshop? A spiritual teacher merely causes what's already within you to rise up into your awareness. You just mentioned hope. Oneness raises up the hope already within."

I looked out the window. "How about this. You said you wanted to know how I got to knowing and living from natural Oneness as the message of Jesus. Do you fish?"

"Love it."

"Good. Would you be willing to meet me at Fish Lake next Tuesday? Is six thirty too early?"

Sam lamented. "Wish I could sleep in—I'm a teacher after all. The sad truth is that I still get up early the whole freakin' summer!"

As we were leaving, I introduced Sam to Margie and Peter. They showered him with genuine interest and kindness, and he knew why I always look forward to seeing them.

I could tell that something was rising up within Sam—something calling out to be remembered—something that was everything.

2
In the Boat: God Is in Everything

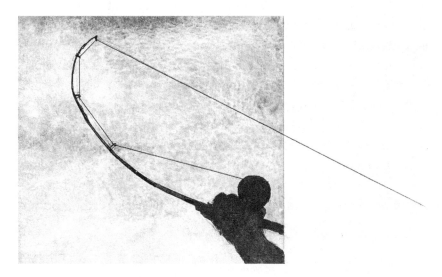

IT WAS A BEAUTIFUL MORNING at Fish Lake when Sam met me at the boat landing. We put my boat into the water and rode into a gorgeous, early-morning fog.

Sam shouted over the hum of the motor, "Let's see if we can persuade some bass to make some poor decisions!"

We rode out to a favorite spot of mine, cut the motor, and began to do our thing. The lake was perfectly quiet, and the water was like glass. It was one of those who-cares-if-a-fish-bites moments.

Then came the pull on Sam's line. By the look of it, Sam had a nice fish. He showed himself to be an experienced fisherman, as he let it run with the bait for a little while and then skillfully brought his catch into my waiting net. It was a good-sized bass, and Sam released it back into the water.

"Sam, this is why I brought you out here—to feel the pull on your line, the grasp of the fish, the quick response. *That* was the feeling I had from my soul when I was being led to live from Oneness."

"You're going to have to help me out here, Tim," Sam said, shaking his head.

"This new spiritual journey I set out on at fifty-nine began with hearing this inaudible voice within me, telling me that there is more than the message of the Church and Christianity. That it was time. I was ready and open enough. There was something already planned and in motion for me. My job was to show up, be open, and pay close attention to what would be coming my way.

"Actually, I learned quickly that the inner voice isn't much of a conversationalist. What I was picking up on was more like: More. Time. Ready. Open. Attention. At first I was being pulled toward books about a broader, more inclusive spirituality. I'd look on Amazon and just pay attention to what my soul was attracted to. I would feel a tug of my soul toward this or that book. I began reading books that were collectively teaching me:

> *You already have within you what you seek and need.*
> *You are the Love of the Divine in your essence.*
> *We come to know God in ourselves, and ourselves in God.*

"Well, we don't talk like that in church!" I said as I sat back.

"Yeah, I don't remember hearing anything like that," Sam responded.

"That tug of my soul felt like that pull on the line that you just felt. As if my soul was grabbing hold of what it was attracted to," I said. "It would grasp something and just run with it, with great joy, like my soul was saying, 'Yes! Now I remember. I already know that! *That's* what I need!' That reaction really intrigued me. I wondered where that was coming from. I thought what I was reading was *new* stuff for me, so I couldn't figure out why a particular book or sentence would just grab me and lure me in. Why *that* one and not another? It felt like when you go somewhere you've never been, and you feel like you've been there before. You remember it for some reason you can't explain."

I paused and looked down into the water. "I began to realize my soul knows much more than I was aware of. So I wanted to find out what else it knows. I read the mystics. I studied the Tao Te Ching, the Bhagavad Gita, Sufism (the mystical arm of Islam), the Kabbalah (Jewish mysticism), *A Course in Miracles*, to name a few. I wanted to see what else resonated with my soul. I visited communities I had no experience with—Buddhist, Hindu, Baha'i, Muslim, Quaker—and meditation centers. I studied Aramaic, the language Jesus spoke and taught in. That opened up many things that my soul resonated with so deeply. His teachings are seen in a much different light in Aramaic.

"With each experience and each book, I could feel the hunger of my soul! Like it was taking in food that it loved and had been missing for so long. Now I feel satisfaction in my soul, even though it's still hungry for more!"

I laughed. "I even met with a lovely group of atheists, who interestingly enough meet regularly on Sunday mornings, religiously. Who knew? I thought one of the perks of being an atheist was that you have Sunday mornings free!"

"Ha! Good one!" laughed Sam.

"But my journey is mine, and yours is yours," I said, looking up at Sam. "What my soul is attracted to at any given point may be quite different from what draws your soul."

Then I asked Sam to look around at the beautiful setting we were in—the lake, the trees, the sounds of the birds, the blue sky above, the clouds moving—and notice what naturally drew him in. As Sam looked around, where his eyes settled and the smile that arose on his face showed what he was thinking. "The water draws me in—and that lone crane standing on the water's edge over there."

"Trust your inner voice, Sam, your inner knowing. Your soul knows what it is attracted to. It knows what speaks to it at this point in its evolution and journey. It also knows what it needs to let go of, what no longer serves it. Like our precious opinions, what we think we know, what we're so convinced of. There are things we need to let go of, in order to live sensitively enough to hear the subtle stirrings of the soul, that 'still, small voice' the Psalmist in the Bible speaks of."

I looked up and saw the sun's reminder of the time that had passed. "It's also about *timing*. What works for me now wouldn't have worked until I was fifty-nine. What the soul is attracted to changes as the soul evolves. That's how I've learned to see it."

"Okay," Sam followed up, "but you brought me all the way out here at six thirty in the morning for that? Couldn't you have just told me?"

I laughed. "I love the first teaching of the Tao Te Ching, the Chinese wisdom written about twenty-four hundred years ago. 'The Tao that can be told is not the eternal name.' Spiritual truth is not something that can be merely told or can even be put into words, as if it is information. The mind can't understand it or grasp it. It can only be known through experience. That's been part of the problem with the Church and Christianity. Different branches of the Church have tried to convince people that they are the only ones with the 'right' information about God and what to believe. Leaders and pastors of my time were trained to be purveyors of religious information, of right thinking.

"And I've noticed that, after hearing what I have to say these days about Oneness, some Church people go right here," I said, pointing to my head, "to the place the Church has taught them to go. I see them get frustrated because they try to *understand* it with their minds. I see them try to figure out, 'Do I agree or disagree? Do I like or dislike that?' But it's not about agreeing or liking. It's about simply letting the inherent Oneness be and letting it speak *on its own terms*. It's really hard for people to do that. We're so used to living in our heads, we don't even realize it."

Sam laughed. "So if someone's telling me I'm out of my mind, it's a compliment?"

"Sometimes!" I grinned. "Especially when it comes to knowing your soul's truth. There is a place for the mind in all of this, as well. The trick is learning to use the mind to *serve the soul*. I'm talking about being intentional about what we're taking into our minds, and hosting thoughts that feed the soul."

Just then a large-mouth bass jumped out of the water in search of its prey. "It's like feeding the body, Sam. You give it what it hungers for. After spending all those years in the Church, with all its requirements and hoops to jump through in order to be 'in a right relationship with God' as the Church puts it, my soul is hungry—just like yours, Sam. It's hungry for what it has already tasted and knows at some level—hungry for anything about its greatest truth, its Oneness with God and with everything else. So I'm intentional about taking into my mind anything about Oneness. Then I set the intention of using my mind to feed my soul phrases or mantras about Oneness."

We watched the fish's ripple effect fade away on the water. "What do you think your soul is hungry for right now, Sam?"

"Not sure," Sam said, looking off onto the surface of the water.

"Listen deeply, Sam, to the hunger pangs."

Sam closed his eyes and slowly looked up from his little rendezvous with his soul. "Peace."

"Your soul is hungry for peace. Feed it, Sam. Pay attention to what your soul needs. It is still maturing and learning, just like everyone else's. Listen to what your soul is asking for as it evolves. It knows where to find it."

Taking in our surroundings, I thought of how I wanted to end this lesson on my boat. "What we humans call 'God' can be known only in experience. The experience of God I'm talking about is not anything out of the ordinary. It's not reserved only for mystics or gurus sitting on top of mountains in the Himalayas. For me, it's in a very ordinary experience of life. It's known in our remembering."

"Remembering?"

"Here's what I mean. There are ordinary experiences in life that trigger our soul's innate knowing or memory. That memory then rises up into our awareness. We remember what we truly are, and it's that awareness that makes all the difference in how we live."

"Okay. What you just said makes sense to me, but I'm not sure why or how."

"That's okay, Sam. Remember, I used the word 'experiences.' It's through profoundly simple experiences that we remember. Like being here! Let's just be here for a bit."

So that's what we did.

———

After we pulled the boat out of the water, I looked over to the west, beyond the trees. "Sam, there's a place where I do some of my best remembering. Could we meet at the playground at Fish Lake Elementary? I love to bring my grandkids there. Does Friday work for you?"

"Sure. Love that playground! I used to bring my kids there. See ya Friday."

3

At the Playground: I Remember

SCHOOL WAS OUT FOR THE summer, but the playground remained a hot spot for the neighborhood kids. I waited for Sam to arrive, and then we walked up to the bench where I usually sit. One of the parents I often see waved to me from across the playground.

"Hi, Tim!"

"Hi, Deb!" I yelled back. Then one of the children waved to me.

"Another one of your *Cheers* places, Tim?"

"This is where I bring my grandkids, Sam. They love it here. Our granddaughter, Olivia, said to me the other day, 'Look at all my friends, Bapa!' I love how children of all different backgrounds connect so naturally."

We watched a little longer. "Ever notice, Sam, how adults who don't know each other act when there are children present? Adults of different races, ethnicities, politics, religion, no religion, different cultures, economic status—all that disappears around the children, and the adults easily become a community, if only for a few, precious moments."

Sam nodded. "It's like the children absorb all of that into themselves and say to the adults, 'We can help you put all that in perspective.'"

I returned the nod. "Awesome. Love it!" I noticed that many of the children who were there that day were very young. "Just look at those toddlers."

We sat together for a while, and then I asked Sam, "Just notice what you're feeling. Do you feel yourself drawn to them in any way?"

After a few minutes, Sam said, "I was just thinking about the moments I first held Ben and Avery after they were born."

"Oh my! Magical. No words, Sam."

"No words. It's always magical, but there's something unique about holding your first child. I remember taking Ben into my arms for the first time. We were staring into each other's eyes. 'Hi, Ben! Hi, little guy. I'm your father!'"

Tears welled up in Sam's eyes as he shook his head. "Everything changed. Me, life, how I saw things. Everything. I realized my life wasn't really *my* life. It wasn't about me anymore. It never really was. I felt a love I didn't know I was capable of knowing. I felt a connection with him that I'd never felt before."

I had to take a moment, because Sam's words brought me back to my own experience as a father. There we were, two fathers sitting on a playground bench, reliving the moments we first realized the wonder of life. It took looking into the eyes of a tiny baby to realize what *our lives* were all about.

I turned to Sam. "What you just described is why I come here. What else do you see?"

Sam observed for a couple of minutes. "Well, I see the same innocence, sweetness, vulnerability that I saw in Ben and Avery."

"Anything else?"

"They love more unconditionally than most adults I know—accept each other. And they're just out here to have fun, to be happy."

Then after taking it all in, Sam said, "I wish the world was more like this."

"I love what our five-year-old grandson, Soren, said to me: 'The Universe is a pool of love.' I should add that he also talks about all the ordinary things that five-year-old boys talk about."

Sam laughed. "I've had one of those!"

"We all are love in our *essence*, Sam," I said, never taking my eyes off of the children. "That's still true for adults. How much that love is realized varies according to the evolution of each soul and the environment the soul is born into. As you know so well, we get the clearest view of that essence in children during the first couple of years of life. Then what the soul is here to work on, how it needs to grow, begins to appear more and more. You can see all of that out here."

Sam pointed to my arm. "I noticed your tattoo before, but I never paid attention to what it says."

"Ah yes. At the age of sixty-seven, I walked into a tattoo parlor for the first time and had this tattooed on my right forearm: '*You are love.*' I did it as a reminder to myself, and to everyone who sees it, what we really are at our core. What we are all here to discover and grow into, our true identity. What you just experienced here is a remembering of your truth, your true identity. Our little three-year-old granddaughter Olivia expressed a profound remembering one day. Out of the blue she said, 'You come from love, and love is for everyone. ' She helped me remember that's why I feel my deepest joy and fulfillment when I'm either loving or being loved."

Looking back at the children, I told Sam, "Being told we *should* be more loving doesn't produce more love. But when we start to see that love is our true nature, we can know love for what it is—natural. Love just happens without our even thinking about it. Love can become like our breathing."

A couple of kids were arguing about who's turn it was, and I smiled. "Obviously there is a lot within us that *isn't* love yet. *Yet* is the operative word, because everything is moving toward its fulfillment in love. But the essence of our truth always remains. You're seeing yourself in these kids and in Ben and Avery. You're seeing your own innocence, unconditional love, joy, sweetness, and vulnerability reflected back to you and rising up into your awareness.

"Sam, you're experiencing your own Divinity. That's why you're being drawn to them. Like is being attracted to like, you could say. They're helping you remember."

Sam observed, "It's like we're saying to them, 'Thank you. I got so caught up and lost in doing this adult thing, that I forgot.'"

"You're also remembering the truth of reality. Not the reality humans sometimes create, but the truth of the fundamental nature of reality! I dare say, we just experienced God."

Sam noticed a mom nursing her baby, a blanket draped over her shoulder protecting a tender moment that was only theirs to know. "When I first held Ben and Avery, I was feeling this, 'I *know you.* I just met you, but I *know that I know you,*' and I didn't have any idea where that came from."

"I get it, Sam. I want to talk about that with you sometime. There's a reason for it, I believe."

Sam watched the kids running, jumping, and giggling together. "God. This Oneness is all so beautiful and such a mystery." Then he turned to me. "What is God?"

I got out my phone and showed Sam a picture of my grandson, Soren. "This child also said to me, 'God is a puzzle of the Universe that goes on forever.' I remember looking at him, thinking, "Whoa! Little guru! You know *that?*"

I smiled. "Time to get back in the boat and talk about how great the great mystery is."

On the way over to Sam's car, we set up our second trip to Fish Lake, and I gave Sam what I called a remembering assignment: "Listen to some music, Sam, and pay attention to what's going on within you."

"What kind of music?"

"Whatever moves you."

4
Back in the Boat: God Is One

WHEN SAM AND I ARRIVED back at Fish Lake, we were like a seasoned team. The boat was in the water in no time. As we rode out to our spot, I asked Sam over the sound of the motor how the music-remembering assignment had gone.

"I listened to Journey, U2. Love their stuff."

"Did you notice what was going on inside?"

"My energy picked up."

"We live so much in our head, Sam. In music, we remember that we're energy. Music we love is energy resonating with our own energy."

Sam, the science guy, said, "Energy needs to move. I can feel music helping my mood's energy resolve itself."

We talked about how music can elevate us to the higher vibrations of love, joy, hope, and peace.

Sam said, "I love the Maya Angelou quote, 'People will forget what you said, people will forget what you did, but people will never forget how you made them feel.'"

"It seems that relationships are primarily energy exchanges, Sam. That's what has the greatest effect. All the more reason to take care of our energy."

———————

When we got to our spot on the water, I cut the motor. "Sam, I want to thank you for being open to what we've been talking about. I appreciate it, and I hope it all triggers something in you. If not, that's okay. I'm having a nice time with you either way."

I then asked Sam to swish his hand around a bit in the water. "Now take a drink from your water bottle and feel the water in your mouth and throat as you swallow. Try and feel the water in your stomach."

Then I looked into the water. "Now, imagine two fish below us. One swims up to the other and says, 'My friends are telling me about this thing called water. They say that I should *believe* certain things about it. But I don't know if I even *believe* in water.' The other fish looks at him through her loving eyes and says, 'Oh, my dear friend. You're in it. It's all around you and within you. You're One with it. You *are* it. You can't not be. Water is much more than something to believe in. You are living it, and it is living itself in you.'

"The Church, with some exceptions, is like the friends of the first fish. It tries to tell people what they should believe *about* the water, that is, God. But the teachings of Jesus are about letting people know—or remember—that they're already swimming in the water, that they *are* the water. Jesus taught people to *know and live from their Oneness with God, that they are living in God, that God is within them.*"

I looked down at Sam's hand, still in the water. "Sam, is water always wet?"

"Of course it is."

"Can wetness separate itself from water?"

"No."

"So it is with you and the Divine, Sam. That's the way it always has been. Always will be. It can't be any other way. It's only a matter of our *awareness* of that truth."

I looked down at the water again. "Sam. Put your hand back in the water. Do you *believe* in water?"

"I suppose, but it's not really a belief. The water is right there. I *know* it!" Sam looked at his hand in the water, and looked around at the rest of the lake. "I'm in it. It's everywhere."

"And *that* is what I believe Jesus was leading people to realize. I believe he wanted everyone to grow into and live from that kind of knowing, as much as possible as a human being."

"Why do you believe that?"

I looked at the setting we were in and continued, "This will probably feel like an unexpected turn, but I need to go to the Lord's Prayer with you now."

"You're right—didn't see that one coming."

"What most people aren't aware of is that there was a tradition at the time of Jesus. Rabbis, spiritual teachers, would summarize the essence of their teaching for their students and followers. That summary was in the form of a prayer. That is what we have in what came to be known as the Lord's Prayer. So it is really important to pay attention to this summary of the essence of his teachings."

"Makes sense."

"And there's no greater way to learn what someone was teaching than to go to the language they taught in."

"Also makes sense," Sam affirmed.

"Jesus spoke and taught in Aramaic, the common language of his people. In Aramaic, the name for God means One, Oneness, Unity. God is the One energy flowing in all that is, connecting everything and enabling it to become what it already is. In the beginning of the Aramaic Lord's Prayer, Jesus creates an image of everything coming out of the interior of the One. Now, the energy that comes out of the interior of the Source, the One, is the same as the Source energy itself. In other words, Jesus is teaching that all is One. He's teaching that everything *is* the One, in its essence—including you, me, and everyone."

I looked out over the lake. "If I were to summarize what Aramaic scholar Dr. Neil Douglas-Klotz has shared with me on the Lord's Prayer in Aramaic, and in Revelations of the Aramaic Jesus, it would be: *Fathering, Mothering of the Universe, your Oneness flows within all that you have given life.*"

I let Sam sit with that for a while. "Sam, in the beginning of the Lord's Prayer, Jesus is teaching everyone to return to the Oneness, the Oneness of all that is. Return, remember, and live from there. Return, remember, and live from there."

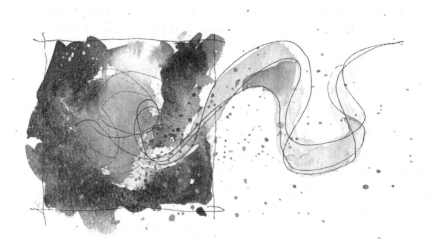

"When I took in the image of everything coming out of the One and naturally being One, my soul loved it. I felt like my soul was saying, 'This is what I was longing for! This is what I already know!' I felt my soul's joy and freedom as it ran with the truth. It felt like coming home. I remembered *the* fundamental truth of all reality."

Sam turned to the water. "Therein lies the answer for this divided world."

"Indeed, Sam. Therein lies the healing for this fearful, divided world we are all swimming in."

Sam sat back in the boat. "Whoa! I gotta sit with that for a while."

I laughed. "Go ahead. You've got eternity!"

After some time passed, Sam said, "That's what I was experiencing at the workshop when you were talking about Oneness. My soul was being touched by your words, and it was drawn toward the Oneness it already knows."

We sat quietly for a while. "Sam, what do you think is the nature or essence of this Oneness, this spiritual energy?"

"I think it's love."

"Yes—pure, *unconditional* love. And if any of us questions whether or not our Source is unconditional love, we need only look at ourselves, because our souls came out of this energy. Sam, what do you want and need more than anything?"

Sam smiled. "Love. Well, that and a fish on my line."

"That's for sure, Sam! What *kind* of love do you need? Conditional love that depends on how well you do? Or unconditional love?"

"Unconditional love, of course."

"It's interesting that you seem so sure about that. And why do you think you need it so badly?" I asked.

"Because that's what my soul came out of."

"Yes! How does unconditional love feel to you?" I asked.

Sam's eyes gazed into the water again. "It feels like taking a drink, after I've been thirsty for a long time."

"Oh, that's a great way to describe it."

Sam let his eyes settle on that lone white crane, standing so contentedly near the shore. "When I have experienced unconditional love, it's also felt like coming home."

"Beautifully said, Sam. And we're all somewhere on the homesick spectrum. Whether we're aware of that being what we're longing for or not."

"*That's* what I was feeling when I was looking at the kids and connecting with them—our Oneness with the One and each other. I already knew about that connection."

"Exactly. Your soul's knowing is simply helping you to *remember* that you're connected. You've always been connected and always will be. It can't be any other way. Remember what you were saying about holding Ben and Avery? What you said about the children at the playground? You saw their innocence, sweetness, vulnerability, joy, unconditional love, and acceptance. But it wasn't just *theirs* you were seeing, Sam. You were experiencing *your own truth* in all those wonderful things rising up within you, as you looked at the children."

"So Tim, that whole water thing you were doing before—you were telling me that I'm already in the water. We're all swimming in the Oneness, the Oneness of God, even when we're not aware of it."

"Yes, Sam."

"But how can I be *aware* of the water—or God?"

"How we can become aware of the Presence is a great question, Sam. Maybe it's the most important question, because being aware is what makes life fun, even magical. It's what makes all the difference in how we actually live."

I looked down into the water and then back to Sam. "God is in you and in all that is. God is a living energy that can only be known as it moves in the world, through the experiences we have. God is in what rises up from our soul into our awareness as we have our life experiences."

I turned back in the direction of the playground. "I come to *know* God in the experience of remembering. At the playground, you were remembering. There is an underlying, constant hum of the Presence as I like to call it, that we can become more and more aware of. But mostly that's what we have as humans—moments of remembering."

Sam was looking into the water, and I let him be still for a bit. He looked up and asked, "You spoke earlier of all the qualifiers or hoops we're taught to jump through in the Church, to be okay with God, or whatever. What were you referring to?"

"I was referring to the Church's teaching that Jesus had to die on the cross so God could accept us as we are. That we have to believe the right things about him. That we need to be baptized, take communion, go to church on Sunday, confess that we're sinners. Many people believe they have to be good enough to get into heaven. All of that."

"Something in my soul knew the truth. Something in *you* knows the truth, Sam. Something in you knows there are no hoops, religious or otherwise, that you have to jump through to be what you already are—one with the Oneness."

Sam smiled. "That's why you speak so much about Oneness and remembering."

"Yep, that's why."

"You know, as a teacher, there are those special moments when I can see the light bulb come on in a student. Their whole face says, 'Yeah, I get what you're saying!' Well, I just had my own moment! I get what you're saying about Oneness—through physics. In quantum physics, there is something bizarre called quantum entanglement. The idea is that the quantum state of a particle cannot be described independently of the quantum state of other particles. They remain connected and continue to affect each other even when separated by vast distances. I've been thinking of God as a separate being. You know, as in 'Our Father who art *in heaven.*' But God is much more than that," Sam said looking up at the sky.

"Wow! That's amazing. Thank you for that, but I have no idea what you just said, Sam!"

"That's okay! I don't understand it either. No one really does!"

"I'm no scientist, Sam, but to me, science is the human attempt to understand how the One expresses itself in the physical realm. You're every bit the teacher of God as I am, Sam."

Suddenly Sam looked like he had an epiphany. "What we call 'God' isn't just involved with the world or life. God *is* the world. God *is* life!"

I smiled. "You're gonna love this one, Sam. Our granddaughter, Olivia, said, 'Love is a scientific word because we're all connected.'"

"Wow, that's amazing!"

"And you have your beautiful Ben and Avery as your spiritual teachers."

After a long pause, Sam slowly said, "Yes I do! But part of me still wonders. How do you know that all of that is actually God?"

"I can't talk you into knowing that it actually is the Divine in you. Only the Divine, the Oneness within us, can convince us of itself."

I waited a bit and followed with, "Whatever emerges from Source is the Source from which it emerges. It *is* the Oneness. It *is* love. And that is everything, because everything emerges from Source."

"You're saying I'm God now?" Sam looked at me incredulously.

"Spiritual teachers sometimes use the analogy of a spark. We are a *spark* of God, they teach. A spark is not the whole fire, just a tiny portion of it. But a spark is still the fire, and it has great potential to grow into something much larger."

"Okay, that makes sense, Tim."

"Let it be whatever it is for you at this point in time, Sam. We've covered things here that I've been sitting with for many years."

Realizing all that had just transpired, I said, "Well, that's enough for today, my friend. You know Bentley Woods not too far from here?"

"Oh yeah."

"There's a clearing in the woods about a half mile from the parking lot. Just follow the trail, and I'll meet you in that clearing. There are some things I'd like to talk about with you there. Next Tuesday morning okay with you—nine a.m.?"

"Works for me."

"Sam, I want to give you another remembering assignment to help you remember your truth. During the next week, focus on being kind, every chance you get during your normal day. Notice what's going on within you when you're kind. That's it. Simple. We'll talk about it on Tuesday."

"Sounds good."

5

In the Woods: Being a Part of God

I SPENT THE WEEK PLAYING with our grandson, Soren, and our grand-daughter, Olivia. I watched the children play—and remembered. When Olivia said, "Bye bye, teeter totter," as we left the playground, and when Soren waved at people he didn't know, I was being reminded of my truth.

I was thinking about all of this as I parked the car and walked toward the clearing in the woods where I would meet Sam. I recalled the beautiful words of William Wordsworth from his *Ode: Intimations of Immortality from Recollections of Early Childhood*:

Our birth is but a sleep and a forgetting:
The Soul that rises with us, our life's Star,
Hath had elsewhere its setting,
And cometh from afar:
Not in entire forgetfulness,
And not in utter nakedness,
But trailing clouds of glory do we come
From God, who is our home:
Heaven lies about us in our infancy!

I've felt his words grounding me here on earth. As a pastor, I watched people of all ages making their way through this world. I observed that Wordsworth had it right in his lovely poem. Life is a kind of knowing and forgetting, and then there can be a remembering.

Life on earth begins with a certain kind of knowing. I thought about the children that Sam and I watched at the playground. I thought about our conversation about these souls, having come so recently from the Oneness, bringing us together despite our differences. Adults who have become attached to politics, religion, race, country, and culture nevertheless become an instant community around these little ones, if only for a few precious moments. I thought about what Sam so wisely observed at the playground, how the children seem to be saying to us, "We can help you put all of that into perspective."

And then life involves some forgetting. As I walked, I remembered how Wordsworth's poem continues:

Shades of the prison-house begin to close
Upon the growing Boy,
But he beholds the light, and whence it flows,
He sees it in his joy;
- - -
At length the Man perceives it die away,
And fade into the light of common day.

We all must start the journey of discovering a "me" that is separate from "them." If we are to make it in this world, we have to think of ourselves as separate beings. We spend the middle years of our lives working and collecting what we think we need. It's all perfectly normal and human, but in the process, the natural connections we knew as little ones become blocked and fade away.

The middle years can play a trick on us. We try to turn dependence into independence, and often believe we've actually pulled it off. We try to turn vulnerability into self-sufficiency. That natural sense of wonder that accompanied us here is replaced by the daily routine.

I then heard a little rustle in the trees to my right. I turned and realized I had been so lost in thought that I hadn't noticed a fawn standing near me. In her little face I saw myself again. I thought about how life can bring a remembering of our truth. This remembering visits us from time to time in those middle years. Most of the time it comes when we least expect it or want it—when we are vulnerable or feel defeated, when we are left wide open to life.

But if we *choose* to age in a way that serves us, we experience a returning that can bring a deeper remembering. The masks of our illusions are removed, and we can see again the true face of reality. Self-sufficiency is unmasked to reveal a vulnerability that was always there. Personal accomplishment is seen for what it always was—succeeding because of the collective efforts of many.

Our wonder at life that we knew as children can return in the form of wonder at the life we have lived. We can be free to walk lighter, as we did when we were a child. We can let go of what we spent decades grasping and holding on to in those middle years of illusion, and we can once again simply be. All the forgetting we've done only makes the remembering that much sweeter and transforming, if we so choose.

———

I got to the clearing in the trees, which was a lovely, open meadow of grass. I picked a spot and put down the blanket I had brought, welcoming one who I knew was fast becoming a dear friend.

I saw Sam coming down the path through the woods.

"Hi, Sam! How's life?"

"Good. I had the kids for the past few days. I always love it in the summer when we can just hang out together. We went to the wave pool and an amusement park."

"What's it like bringing Avery to those places?"

"She's super social. She just starts talking to anyone near her. She connects really fast, and people are often drawn to her."

Sam paused as he focused on the meadow. "I've learned so much from her. Sometimes I think, 'Who is the challenged one? Avery, or me?' I admire her for that. The connections she makes often wouldn't be happening without her initiating them. Of course, you have to keep an eye on things. She can go too far sometimes."

Sam asked me how I was. "I was sitting here in this open space thinking about how good it feels to be part of something bigger than myself." I turned to Sam. "When have you known that feeling?"

"You feel that in team sports," Sam said as he looked off into the clearing. "This past year there was this student at my school who needed a wheelchair-accessible van, and the students got together and raised the money the family needed. I was able to be a part of that, and yeah, it was amazing—so cool to see the whole school come together like that."

"I love hearing stories like that, Sam. Yes! The soul innately knows it is part of something much bigger than itself. So when it has an experience like being in a team sport or raising money for someone's van, the soul lets you know its truth in the good feeling you have. It can expand beyond the confines of the body and the smallness of the ego. The soul can leave the cramped space and energy it's been in, spread its wings, fly into its truth—and we remember."

I noticed some tears welling up in Sam's eyes as I spoke. "Sometimes love is welcomed by our tears. Why do you think that is, Sam?"

Taking in the open clearing, Sam said, "I think there are tears sometimes when we see something that reminds us of the openness and spaciousness of our heavenly home. We all need the feeling of being able to breathe."

"I love that, Sam! At the same time, I love when spiritual teacher Shai Tubali cautions us of only thinking of our true home as off in a distant heaven somewhere. He says, 'If God is everywhere, then this is our home too.'"

We paused a bit to take in our surroundings.

"As humans, we're not built to remember all the time, Sam. We have moments here on earth, experiences of remembering. But we can create more moments of remembering than we are often aware of."

After spending some time quietly taking in the meadow, I asked Sam, "So, the kindness assignment I gave you—how did it go? By the way, I didn't mean to give you the impression you're not a kind person. I was just suggesting that you be intentional about it."

"I know. Being intentionally kind was pretty cool. I started out thinking that I'd have to *look* for opportunities to be kind, but I was reminded that the nature of life is such that it naturally brings those opportunities to you. I never really paid much attention to that before."

Sam started to tell me something and then hesitated, as if it wasn't important enough. "I went to the gym the next day, and an elderly woman held the outside door open for me. And there was this simple moment when we smiled at each other. It made me want to return the favor and hold the inside door for her. That created another moment when I felt a connection and something coming to life in me. It's something I've probably done a thousand times, but I've never paid attention to what was happening within me.

"So I spent the rest of the week intentionally smiling wherever I went. When a smile was exchanged, it felt like we were helping each other remember that there is love in the world. Hang in there. It's going to be okay. It was like we were offering each other our divinity. Then I focused on sending kindness out through my eyes when I smiled. Whether the person noticed or not, I felt my own self healing."

"Thanks Sam. That's become my new and favorite hobby—looking for and spotting the divine in people, and in life, as I go about my day. And isn't it beautiful how life has its own natural way of helping us remember our truth? When someone is kind to us, we can feel the kindness already within ourselves rising up. We naturally want to return the kindness. We wonder if God is real. We may ask, 'How can I actually know or experience God, and not just try and believe there is one?' That kindness rising up within you, that's God, Sam! It can be that simple. If you ever doubt that you are love, just be kind. Let life help you remember. And when you know that feeling, Sam, be with it for a while. Marinate in it, and let it do its work on you. Let it help you remember that this is your natural habitat."

I turned to the clearing. "This may seem random, but what's it like inside your head, Sam?"

He rolled his eyes, spinning his index finger around. "You don't want to know. Pretty busy!"

"Yeah, me too. It's like a crazy party going on in mine. I hear these thoughts and conversations going on. I move around from one conversation to the other. I listen in and get lost."

I imagined the clearing filling up and getting very noisy. "A few years ago I read about studies in neuroscience. They generally said that we have six thousand thoughts or more going through our minds every day. And something like seventy to ninety percent of those are negative, self-referential, repetitive, or useless. Our brain just keeps spinning the same negative, useless stuff.

"Have you ever just sat and observed your mind, Sam? Just noticed what thoughts pop up on their own? I have, and I think the studies are right. It's crazy in here, Sam," I said, pointing to my head and spinning my finger. "I notice a thought popping up about something, and then all of a sudden, my mind is in Cleveland! Where did *that* come from? And we're the ones allowing ourselves to be taken away by all that."

After a bit, I continued, "It makes sense to me that, in the Aramaic Lord's Prayer, Jesus emphasizes the importance of clearing out."

"Clearing out?"

"You know that part of the Lord's Prayer that says 'Hallowed be thy name?'"

"Sure."

"The Aramaic word Jesus used can be translated 'clear out space,' to remove the clutter in our minds, so that the name—the presence of God already within us—can rise up into our awareness, become more clear, and become the energy we live from."

"Good luck clearing out *my* mind! How do you stop all the thoughts?"

"You don't. I just started practicing what the meditation teachers were telling me. Just observe the thoughts and then, by spending time as the observer, you don't *identify* with the thoughts as much. Just observe and allow them to be, and usually they calm down and loosen their hold on us. I've found that it's like the thoughts just need to be observed, and then they fade away like the fog that was probably here this morning. That's one way I've discovered that I can at least *move toward* decluttering and hallowing out my mind. We'll always have thoughts. That's what the mind is built to do. But the key is not identifying with them."

After a pause, I continued. "I've found that thoughts seem to thrive on lack of observation. It's like they love working undercover. Have you ever been driving somewhere, and all of a sudden you realize you haven't been thinking about your driving at all? You haven't really noticed anything around you the whole way? Your mind has taken you to twenty other places as you're driving along—anywhere but where you are, in your car, at that moment."

"Yeah!" Sam said. "It's scary to think that if I'm driving like that, how many around me are doing the same thing."

"Exactly. We all know we get carried away by our minds to a place we had no real intention of going. Our thoughts are driving us. As meditation teachers often say, our thoughts think us, instead of us thinking our thoughts. I've found that observation is like kryptonite to thoughts. They just seem to lose their strength and fade away, once I pay attention to them."

I scanned the clearing we were in. "Clearing out so the Name, the presence of the One can be more fully remembered and lived. Jesus showed his wisdom when he emphasized that. When I began this journey, I would get up in the morning and intuitively know that I needed to say, 'I know nothing.' I learned to think of my mind as a screen, and I was clearing it by saying that.

"I discovered that I needed to try and go all the way with this. It didn't work for me to say, for example, 'I know lots of things, but there's always more.' I discovered that whenever I said, 'I know,' I could feel myself closing up inside. In telling myself that I already knew, I was actually telling myself that I had no need to take in anything new. Even if I left the door open, I couldn't welcome anything new coming in *as it was*, because I was always comparing it to what was already in my mind, to see how it fit with what I thought I knew. I'm talking here about letting go of my obsession with my head-type of knowing, and instead opening up to the intuitive, soulful kind of knowing deep inside."

After a pause, I looked around the clearing again. "The road to remember is best walked in open space. Experience has shown me that the more open and uncluttered our mind is, the more Spirit is able to work on us. It's like Spirit sees an opening and can bless us in the ways it wants to. There is less interference. That's why I brought you out here. Look around and take a deep breath. What do you feel?"

"I feel like I can breathe. I feel the spaciousness—like the possibilities are endless."

"Oh, I love that, Sam. Endless possibilities. You know, I've found that falling asleep is the moment of endless possibilities."

"Say what?"

"Think about it, Sam. When we're asleep, our consciousness is wide open, passive, not resisting anything. We're not muddying up the waters. I've learned that what we do with those moments when we're falling asleep is crucial. It's been fascinating to see what happens when I say, as I'm falling asleep, 'Spirit, spirit guides, have your way with me. I am open to receive whatever you want to plant within me tonight. I'm all yours.' Then I drift off. The Dalai Lama says that sleep is the best time for meditation. I've found that to be true.

"This is going to sound really weird, but when I get up at night to go to the bathroom, the instant I take a seat, insights sometimes shoot into my awareness. I go 'Wow! That's really interesting!' It's as if Spirit has been working on me, and then I become aware of what has been coming in during the night. This has been going on for decades."

I laughed hard and said, "When I was a pastor, there were so many times I shared in a sermon, or elsewhere, what came to me on the toilet seat. As the words came out, I'd be thinking, 'If you only knew where *that one* came from!' It's like the Universe and I have our own little, private joke. It's so weird and wonderful."

I looked over, and Sam was looking at me like, "What just happened?"

"And those first moments of waking up are so important for establishing how we will live that day. I'm talking about those moments before our crazy roommate wakes up. That's what Michael Singer calls the voice in our head that won't shut up. When you first wake up, you can just be—in that clear, open space that's been created within you during your sleep.

"I often repeat a simple mantra to myself the moment I realize I'm conscious. It's what I told you our granddaughter Olivia said: 'You come from Love, and Love is for everyone.' Then, while I'm still lying down, I see myself going through what I think I'll be doing that day. I see myself being Love, whatever I'm doing—being guided throughout the day by my true Self, instead of by my mind's thoughts. I spend some moments soaking in the energy of what I'm seeing. Other times, I find that fresh insights come into my consciousness as I'm waking up. It feels like, 'Oh! *That's* what you left for me through the night! Thank you!' Even if I'm not aware of anything at that moment, I realize later that I was being worked on in the night."

I realized I had given Sam a whole lot, and we needed to shift things a bit. After a pause, I said, "Let's practice clearing ourselves out in this beautiful, open space by focusing on just being here."

After a while, Sam looked up and smiled. "I've been thinking about how the sun affects us. If our souls emerged from light energy, it seems to make sense that the sun would energize us. It's more Oneness."

"More Oneness, Sam."

I looked over at some trees on the edge of the clearing. "Actually, this is where my ashes are going to be spread—my wife's, too—out here in the open. We think it's a good way to express our freedom when we pass. We love trees. Trees say beautiful things to us all, if we listen."

Sam looked around. "Nice spot."

"You should be here at night, Sam. Want to give it a try?"

"Sure. I don't have the kids this week."

"Okay. Meet me out here at ten Thursday night."

As we were getting into our cars, I said. "Oh, and here's your next remembering assignment: Keep practicing being present, present only to the moment you're in. See you under the stars!"

Part 2

6

Under the Stars: What It All Means

ON THURSDAY NIGHT, I DROVE up to the parking lot near the open space where Sam and I would be taking in the stars. The clear sky was telling me, "You picked a good night for stargazing." We were far enough away from the city that the stars would shine brightly.

I remembered a story I had heard from a pastor I knew. On his way to a Christmas Eve service, he was listening to another pastor give a Christmas sermon on the radio. The pastor was talking about the city lights of Bethlehem, but he accidentally said "the shiny, shitty lights of Bethlehem." He kept saying it over and over, without realizing it. I love that story!

As the remaining daylight guided me to the open space, I thought about how much there is in the Bible that I cannot stand—like violence, patriarchy, and judgment. The Church justifies it and—worse yet—attributes it to God. Even so, there are Bible passages I still enjoy, such as the story of Abraham. God promised to raise up a nation through Abraham, but there were two slight problems: he had no offspring, and he was an old geezer. The plan God had given him wasn't materializing, so Abraham asked God why. God took him outside and told him to consider the stars. God said, "Count them if you can. So will be the number of your offspring."

There is a line at the end of that story that everyone seems to miss. It says "as the sun was going down." God had actually taken Abraham out there in the daylight! Abraham knew the stars were there, even if he couldn't see them at the moment. That little detail reminds us that sometimes we've got to trust our inner knowing, especially when we can't see any evidence at the time.

––––––––––

I sat on the ground for about an hour. By the time Sam arrived, it was darker than the inside of a cow, as my brother-in-law says.

When I saw Sam's flashlight coming toward me, I waved mine, and we had a namaste moment, greeting each other's light. Sam sat down on the grass, and we quickly lost ourselves in the stars.

"How did the being-present assignment go for you, Sam?"

"I loved it, but that's hard to pull off!"

I laughed. "I always say the hardest place to be is where you are."

"I loved it, though. The spinning in my mind subsides, and I'm not as lost in my thoughts. I guess it's because, when I'm present in the moment, I get out of myself."

"I think so, Sam. Being intentionally present in the moment does get us out of the small self we're so obsessed with. It helps us to remember that we're part of something magnificent, something much larger than ourselves. That in itself is comforting. I love what Eckhart Tolle says, 'Focus only on this moment, and tell me what problems you have.' You'll find that, in that moment, you're actually okay. Everything you need *for that moment* is present. Being present helps us remember the truth we're living in at *every* moment."

"What about the really poor, who don't have food or the basics? You can't tell them to just be present and to know that they have everything they need."

"For sure, Sam. But I think the 'focus and realize' thing does work for everyone. Even when we are poor or sick, we can find a point of focus that will take us beyond our small self in that moment. By focusing on something beyond our small self, we let go of our problems and all that weighs us down, even if just in that moment, and we settle into peace. It's there I'd have to say that the present moment can tell us what to do next to help ourselves or someone else."

"What do you think we're doing here, Sam?

"In this place or here on earth?"

"Here on earth."

Sam sighed. "I don't know, really. I'd like to think there's some great purpose or meaning to it all. Something in me says there is."

After we sat with that for a while, I looked up at the stars. "Yeah. I'm pretty sure it has to do with golf," I replied.

Sam started laughing, "According to my nieces, it's all about Taylor Swift!"

I took a long, deep breath, followed by an equally long exhale that seemed to mirror the many decades I've spent pondering the meaning of life. "It makes sense to me that we're here to grow into the love and wisdom we came from. Through the experiences we have. Then we return to that love and wisdom, and the journey of growth continues."

Sam turned to me. "Hmm, when I see what's happening in this world, it seems like a lot of us haven't gotten the memo."

"I know." Looking up at the vastness of the universe, I turned to Sam. "It feels to me like what an acorn is to an oak tree, that's what we are to love. It's all there within us, but we've got a whole lot of growing to do."

After some more stargazing, I laughed. "I've got a friend, Tony, who loves to say, 'I'm not much, but I'm almost all I ever think about.' How true is that? And here we are, two of over eight billion specks on a planet that is a tiny speck in the corner of an ever-expanding universe."

Sam, the science guy, chimed in, "I've heard anywhere from two hundred billion to two trillion galaxies. Scientists now say that at the speed of light, it would take forty-six billion light-years to get to the farthest galaxy. But we can't really know because the universe is expanding. Just try and wrap your mind around the distance light would travel in just *one* year! But how could there even be a farthest galaxy? That would mean, what? That there's nothing beyond it? What would that nothing be?"

"I'm glad we're sitting down, Sam. My head's spinning. I've heard there are more stars in the Universe than grains of sand on all the beaches on earth. Is that really true?"

"True! I've heard some scientists say five to ten times more," the science guy said, "but again, that's just a guess based on what we know—or think we know."

In the quiet, I said,

> *When I look at your heavens, the work of your fingers,*
> *the moon and the stars that you have established;*
> *what are human beings that you are mindful of them,*
> *mortals that you care for them?*
> *Yet you have made them a little lower than God,*
> *and crowned them with glory and honor.*

"Where is that from?" Sam asked, never taking his eyes off the stars.

"The Bible, Psalm Eight. We want to matter, Sam. We *need* to matter. Every soul cries out, 'I matter! I have worth. I have dignity. I am sacred.'"

"That's our knowing of our own glory and honor."

"You got it, Sam. You know, looking up at these stars reminds me of a quote from Rumi: 'I have been a seeker and I still am, but I stopped asking the books and stars. I started listening to the teaching of my Soul.'"

"Oh I love Rumi! Jadyn and I studied his poetry in a class we took together in college. But how do you listen to your soul?"

"I'm still working on that one, Sam. I think it has to do with paying attention to what gives you energy, motivation, and hope—listening to those inner stirrings, promptings. I think it has something to do with how something *feels*. If we feel joyful, peaceful, excited, intrigued, calm, or curious about doing something, then our soul is telling us we're on track. If we get feelings of dread, uneasiness, heaviness, or lack of energy, our soul is cautioning us to back away. Our souls talk to us much more than we realize."

"In our time together, Sam, I've talked as though I know so much. When I look up at the night sky, I find myself right back at 'I know nothing.'"

Never taking my eyes off the stars, I said, "To be honest, sometimes I wonder if they're having a good chuckle, watching me from the other side. 'Oh that Tim!' I imagine them saying, 'Look at him at that workshop, talking like he knows what's what. That's funny! Dear, dear, Tim. With some things you're kind of in the ballpark. When you focus on love, you hit it *out* of the park. Other times? Well, at best you're circling the park looking for a parking spot. Oh Tim, the things you're trying to talk about are so different and so much better than you think.'" I turned to Sam. "Does that bother you when I say that?"

"No, not at all. I understand that, actually," Sam responded.

"Well, I'm just doing the best I can, Sam, living within the limitations of being a human, like everyone else."

"That's what I'm doing, Tim—the best I can. Well, most of the time anyway. I think that's what everyone's doing. With that in mind, we should probably give each other some more slack."

"Good point, Sam. Remember when I was telling you in the boat that when I began this spiritual journey, I had the sense that I was looking for something I already knew?"

"Yeah."

"Circling back to what you were saying about meaning and purpose—we all seem to have an innate need for that. It's not enough for us to just go through the motions. It all has to mean something. It has to have a point. I'm sure you get what I'm saying."

Sam nodded his head, "When I get out of bed in the morning, I sometimes think, 'Why am I doing this?'"

"Makes sense, Sam. There is infinite meaning and purpose within the One that our souls all emerged from—so, in a very real sense, we *are* meaning and purpose in our very being. To me, that's why it hurts so much when we're not conscious of meaning and purpose in our lives. That pain is actually our truth speaking to us, our truth wanting to be known and expressed. We literally *need* to find what gives our unique souls meaning and purpose. Our divinity knows we matter, Sam. We all know the longing of 'Please see me! Please hear me!' Something in us knows we are worthy of being seen and heard. That's our divinity speaking, Sam."

"So, if you want to remember what you are, get in touch with your need for meaning and purpose," Sam observed, never taking his eyes off the stars.

After sitting in the silence for a while, I set my gaze on a lone star. "We know the longing of wanting to be seen and heard. Sometimes that comes from a needy ego, but it's there we are often hearing from our divinity, which knows its worth. As far as finding out what our unique purpose is, there is no end to our learning. But there is one thing we're all here to learn and grow into."

"Love," Sam said, without even thinking about it.

"Exactly!"

Scanning the night sky, I went on, "It's so freakin' humbling being here."

Sam kept looking at the sky. "We all need to be comfortable with mystery, with trust, with humility."

"Amen, my friend. So many people these days go around saying, 'I know. I'm right. You're wrong.'"

Sam responded, "I love what C. S. Lewis wrote in *Mere Christianity*: 'Humility is not thinking less of yourself, but thinking of yourself less.' Out here under the stars, that makes so much sense."

Looking up, I sighed. "The meaning of life. Now there's the most humbling of questions. I've looked to endless sources for that answer, and the answer that resonates the most with me actually came from dead people."

Sam turned to me. "Come again?"

"One of the things I got into when I began this spiritual journey is near-death experiences or NDEs. These come from people who died and crossed over for a certain time, and have come back to talk about it. I've read and listened to hundreds of their stories. I find them fascinating. Even more fascinating to me is how my soul reacts to them. It feels like a homesick traveler getting a letter from home.

"What is actually experienced seems to vary according to what the soul is able and needs to experience. But the vast majority speak of learning that Earth is like a school for the soul. The souls who come back from NDEs still have things to do and learn here. That's why it wasn't their time yet to go to the other side.

"When I took all that in, I felt this soulful thumbs-up, like my soul was saying, 'Yes! I remember that!' When I began to see the wisdom of this being a school for the soul, it really changed my perspective on what we experience here—especially the hard stuff, from which we can learn the most. When we accept that there is nothing more important than the growth of our souls into love and wisdom, then instead of resisting hard things, we can ask the question, 'What's in this experience for me to learn?' We don't see the hard thing as an intruder who broke into our house and is not supposed to be there."

Sam sighed. "Yeah, no one likes the hard stuff in life. I know I don't."

"It's like when you give your students a hard assignment or something hard to read and comprehend. Why do you do that, Sam?"

"I want my students to be challenged. To learn new things—new possibilities for themselves and the world. To discover what they're capable of. That's when they grow the most, if they're willing to dive into it."

"And, Sam, the most universal instinct of everything, from a tiny seed to the Universe, is to evolve, expand, and grow into what it's intended or designed to be."

The science guy nodded. "That's basic science."

"And the message from the other side is that we are *all* here to ultimately grow into the Love and wisdom we emerged from and already are—through the experiences we have here."

"Hmmm. That resonates," Sam said slowly. "Tim, what we're talking about reminds me of Rumi's poem, 'The Guest House.' I first heard it in our philosophy class in college. I loved it so much that I memorized it."

"I love that too! Tell me what you remember."

"Well, let's see:"

> *This being human is a guest house.*
> *Every morning a new arrival.*
> *A joy, a depression, a meanness,*
> *some momentary awareness comes*
> *as an unexpected visitor.*
> *Welcome and entertain them all!*
> *Even if they're a crowd of sorrows,*
> *who violently sweep your house*
> *empty of its furniture,*
> *still treat each guest honorably.*
> *He may be clearing you out*
> *for some new delight.*
> *The dark thought, the shame, the malice,*
> *meet them at the door laughing,*
> *and invite them in.*
> *Be grateful for whoever comes,*
> *because each has been sent*
> *as a guide from beyond.*

"Whoa, great memory! Yes! That's what the ones who cross over and come back are saying. It's all for our growth," I responded. "Tough to be that kind of host, though, isn't it? Tell me, Sam, what was in 'The Guest House' that attracted you so much?"

"I think I was tired of all the drama with my parents and their marriage—tired of fighting it all—tired of all those years of wanting things to be different. Instead, the idea of being welcoming was appealing, I guess."

"Vulnerability is scary," I said looking at a lone star. "Two unwelcome guests visited my house—my life—for an extended stay. As Rumi says, they were emptying my house of its furniture and clearing me out for some new delight. One moved in gradually when I was around forty. I was feeling this increasing sadness that was different from the kind of sadness I had known before—the kind that comes and goes. But this time, I was losing energy, becoming negative, withdrawing into myself. And everything took *so much effort*. It felt like I was walking in lead boots every day. I'd take them off when I fell into bed at night, but I'd wake up the next day, and there they were, back on my feet.

"No matter how hard I tried, I couldn't snap out of it. I couldn't suck it up. None of my usual solutions worked—laughter, golf, prayer, nature, chocolate—nothing. There I was, a pastor who was supposed to help people, shepherd them through life, and I was just stumbling around the pasture myself. I was lost, helpless, and afraid. I was diagnosed with depression."

"Sounds dark."

"The other guest burst in suddenly, some years after the depression. I left my office on the way to a meeting and stepped into the men's room next door. I was standing there doing my thing, and out of the blue, I saw red. I'm a pretty sharp guy, so I figured maybe something wasn't quite right." I looked over at Sam. "See what I mean?"

I continued telling my story to my audience of two—Sam and the lone star. "I went over to my doctor's clinic. They took an MRI and said they'd call. Five hours from the time I made my routine men's room visit, I'm standing in Aisle Six at Target. My phone rings and I hear, 'There's a mass in your bladder. It looks like it's probably cancer.' I don't remember driving home, but when I got there, my wife took one look at me and said, 'What happened?' Five hours and fifteen minutes after my men's room visit, I'm saying to my wife, 'I probably have cancer.'"

I paused for a minute, thinking about how I had watched the stars slowly appear, while I was waiting for Sam to arrive.

"It's amazing how the darkness helps us see the light. It sucked, but the darkness of the depression helped me see the power of vulnerability. I began to see a way out, and learned what I needed to do to help myself—an antidepressant, exercise, eating differently, being mindful, and so on. Eventually I chose to share my depression experience with our congregation in a series of sermons. After I did that, the knocks on my office door began. I heard, 'Me too,' and 'My brother is depressed,' and 'I don't know what to do with my wife's depression.'"

"I could tell they saw a safe place in me—someone who's been there and understands what they were feeling. I never truly saw my ability to help people until I became helpless. I never saw strength for what it is until I became weak.

"The same happened with my cancer experience, which I came through just fine, thankfully. Before, it was always me sitting in the bleachers and cheering on someone who was struggling with cancer in their life. Now I was on their team, and it was a whole new ball-game—one that I was in. Now I listened differently. I could meet them where they were. And they knew it.

"At my retirement, I asked that they name the men's room next to the church office, 'Tengbladder Hall,' and someone actually did put up a paper sign. I said I wanted to bring my grandchildren there some day and say to them, 'This is what the people thought of your grandpa.'"

Sam laughed. "Oh, that we all would be so honored!"

He paused, and then said, "Thanks for not asking me about my divorce, Tim."

"None of my business, Sam." After a moment, I asked, "Do you *want* to talk about it, Sam?"

He took a deep breath. "Yeah, I think I do. Not here though. I just want to soak this all in."

———————

After another ten minutes, we stood up to go back to our cars.

"I'm open to listening, Sam. How about we go back to Ole's Tavern next time?"

Sam nodded his head. "You said you love being there because that's where you can be human. That's what we'll be talking about—being human!"

Sam looked at his calendar. "Next Wednesday? Two p.m.?"

"Fine. Can I give you another remembering assignment?"

"Sure."

"Create something."

"Create something?" Sam looked surprised. "Anything?"

"Anything."

7

Back at Ole's Tavern: When Things Go Wrong

I GOT TO OLE'S TAVERN before Sam did. After greeting Sue, I noticed that my spot under the old Smoke Eater was taken. What? In church, it was like everyone had season tickets to a certain pew—and even to the same spot in the pew. If a visitor sat in their spot, the world was suddenly off kilter.

With my spot taken, I walked over to the bar, where Carl and Cheryl were seated. I started up my usual conversation with Carl.

"How goes it, Carl?"

"Same shit song. Different verse."

"Hang in there. Tomorrow's another day."

"Yeah, that's what I'm afraid of."

"When you want to write a different song, my friend, let me know. I'll try and help. It's a standing invitation."

Carl has become an acquired taste. His honesty sometimes makes me want to say, "Yup, been there." Other times I just put my hand on his shoulder. Either way, we meet in a certain Oneness.

He can be annoying in another way. Sometimes when I look at Carl, it's like looking into a mirror, because I see what annoys me about myself. Making peace with myself is making peace with him. It's another encounter with Oneness. That's why I sometimes talk with Sue about Carl's constructively annoying way. She often says, "Yup, been there," and puts her hand on my shoulder. I smile. More Oneness.

I turned to Cheryl. "How's your daughter holding up?"

"Better lately. Thanks for asking, Tim. I appreciate it."

I love my talks with Cheryl—much love, few words.

Sam walked in and looked around. When he spotted Margie and Peter, he went over to their table. Simply by being themselves, they poured their kindness, gentleness, and love onto him. Fortified with what he needed, Sam sat down next to me.

"Welcome, my friend! How did the remembering assignment go? Did you create?"

Sam looked a little baffled. "I don't know. What I mean is, I play guitar and write songs. I sat down to write and a song just came together quickly. I don't know where it comes from. It's like I'm part of something bigger than myself."

I smiled. "Beautiful. Your soul emerged from the One's creativity. You *are* the One's creativity."

Sam nodded, but seemed a bit nervous.

"You still want to talk about your divorce?"

"Yeah."

"Where would you like to start?"

"Well, it wasn't any one thing. It got complicated," Sam said, looking over at a couple sitting at the bar. "When we got married, everything was good. We were each doing our own thing—me at school and Jadyn at the clinic where she worked. We bought a house and spent time fixing it up. School got more demanding. I got involved in teacher contract negotiations and some coaching. Jadyn became pregnant. Ben came. He was awesome. We loved being parents and all of that, but with everything that was going on, we were paying less attention to each other and our marriage. Less attention to ourselves too. We realized it, but we just didn't have the energy I guess to do anything about it. We just focused on getting up in the morning and doing what we had to do."

Sam exhaled. "Jadyn started talking about feeling alone, neglected, and about losing herself. I wish I had said, 'Me too,' but I didn't. I didn't really make any changes in how I was living. I don't know. I guess I was angry too, and I took it out on her. I don't know.

"About the only thing we did to connect with each other was, well, make love. Which was more like two ships passing in the night. Then Jadyn became pregnant with Avery, and all of her issues were piled on all the ones we already had. Then ..."

Sam took a deep breath and a drink of his beer, as if he was collecting his courage. "And then I let myself get way too close to one of the teachers I was working with." He looked at his beer, as if he was looking for something.

"It started out ... I don't *think* I intended anything inappropriate to happen. We always enjoyed each other, but when the Covid pandemic hit, well, teaching got a whole lot harder. We started Face-Timing, processing, and crying in our beer as they say. I was telling myself I was talking with her because she understood what I was going through, and I knew what she was struggling with. Eventually, I couldn't pretend any longer. I was lying to myself."

Sam noticed a couple sitting at the bar. "And then ... we ... then we had an affair. I knew it was wrong immediately and felt guilty about how exciting it felt. Ashamed, actually. It was so horrible to look at Jadyn and the kids, knowing I was failing them."

Tears started welling up in Sam's eyes. After a minute or so, he continued. "I know it was both of us, Jadyn and me. We were both part of what happened, but man," Sam said, shaking his head, "I was the one who destroyed any chance we had. One day Jadyn asked point blank about me and this person, and I just couldn't hold it in any longer. I told her everything. Shit! I hurt Jadyn so badly! Avery will never know, but Ben deserved to hear the truth from me."

Sam was still crying. "That was beyond horrible. I'll never forget the look on Ben's face. Our relationship is not the same now, of course. I'm trying to give him some time. Maybe someday . . ."

Sam glanced again at the couple at the bar, who now seemed to be in earnest conversation. "I don't think I can ever forgive myself for what I did. I begged Jadyn to forgive me and give us a second chance, but she just couldn't. It was over. Her trust in me was gone. She lost her respect for me. So did Ben. Hell, I did too."

Sam looked over his shoulder a bit, as if he were looking back. "You so desperately want and need a father you can respect. I know what that's like, and I failed my own son!"

Sam closed his eyes and said, "I'd probably do the same as Jadyn, if the situation were reversed. Jadyn's got her stuff, like all of us, but she is a wonderful person. She's a great mom, and I blew it. Threw it all away. I just can't forgive myself."

Sam turned to me. "But God does, right?"

I looked Sam in the eye and said something that totally surprised him. "No, I don't believe God forgives any of us."

"No? What?"

"What I mean is, I don't believe that God forgives, because God never judges in the first place. If there's no judgment, there is no need for forgiveness or need to ask for it. Sam, if someone does something wrong to you and then comes to you to say, 'Please forgive me,' and if you never judged them for it, what would *you* say to them?"

"I'd probably say, 'Let it go. Don't let it be a barrier between us.'"

"Exactly. And that's from an imperfect human! With God, we're talking about absolutely perfect, unconditional love, as in no conditions. Love has no interest in judging or need to judge. Love doesn't need you to come and say how sorry you are and grovel for forgiveness. Love's only interest is in what you *learned* from the experience."

"Hmm. That rings true, Tim. When Ben or Avery mess up, I want to know what they learned from it. I love them, and I want to know how they will handle the situation in the future."

"It's we humans who judge, Sam, so forgiveness is a need in human relationships. When we forgive ourselves, ask someone for forgiveness, or forgive someone else, the relationship is healed and restored.

"None of that exists in God's relationship with us, because from God's perspective, the Oneness never ceases. Sam, I've been taught that there's something that's referred to as a *life review*, when we cross over to the other side."

"Oh, is that where you see your whole life flash before you?"

"Yeah, something like that. We are given a chance to see the life we just lived. Did we take advantage of this or that situation to learn and grow? Or not? That's the point of the review, because that's the point of life here in Earth School. The life review is not done in a spirit of judgment. It's for your benefit. There is no judgment on the other side—only the ongoing journey of growing into love and wisdom."

After giving Sam a moment, I asked, "What did you learn from the divorce, Sam?"

Sam looked out the window. "I learned that I can be awfully foolish, but I already knew that."

He turned to me, "I ended up getting an apartment. I packed up my stuff, and the day I left was the worst day of my freakin' life. I stood at the door, looked back, and knew the life I had was gone. Because of me, mostly. Even though I knew I'd still be coming back to get the kids for my time with them, I knew I could never really go back. What had been was gone. I got into my car and drove off with my home in the rearview mirror. That's the worst feeling in the world," Sam said, shaking his head, "especially when you know you did it to yourself."

After giving Sam the time he needed, I put my hand on his arm. "I'm so sorry."

Another question followed another pause. "Sam, what was it like for you going through the separation and divorce?"

"It totally sucked, especially at first. Sitting there in my stupid apartment. Beating myself up. Going to pick up the kids—that felt so weird, like I was a visitor in my own home. It was like I had left, locked myself out, threw away the key, and had no way to get back in."

"Hmmm. The key. Where is a key, Sam? You're maybe far enough along with the divorce to try a new perspective."

"Ha! What the hell could that be?" Sam asked, exasperated.

"What I'm going to say doesn't fix the past. It doesn't take the pain away. But then again, that's the point of what I'm talking about."

"I was hoping for some magic pill you might have, Tim."

"Sam, we all have an idea of what we think our lives are *supposed to be*, and none of it involves anything difficult. That's our ego's perspective—nothing difficult, please. Our egos want control. Two people marry, and they think they'll stay together forever. Nobody marries so they can get a divorce. As a pastor, I probably married five hundred couples, and I never saw that in anyone's marriage plan."

"Hell, no!" Sam said.

"A child is born, and they're not *supposed* to be born with any challenges, like Down syndrome. Any one of us is born, and we're supposed to live a long, healthy life. And when someone dies young, we decide that they left us too soon. I saw it hundreds of times as a pastor.

"But here's what I've learned. All of this is for the growth of our soul into its inherent love, strength, and wisdom. We're not here only for smooth sailing. We're not here only to be comfortable. Nor is God the one who is supposed to keep things that way, even though in the Church we are constantly asking God to fix this, take that away, or keep us from something we don't want to experience."

I continued, "Tony Robbins says that 'life is always happening *for you*, not *to you*.' That resonates with me. It's clear to me that my soul knows that's true, at some deep level."

I let Sam sit with this for a while, trying to see how he was reacting. He looked like a student in trouble, getting a lecture from the principal—like he was saying, "Crap! That's the best you've got? I'm looking for a way out of this shit!"

I pressed on. "As I said, the way our souls grow is through the experiences they have here. There is no other, easier way. We grow from good experiences and hard experiences—*especially* the hardest. That's the set-up here. That's the nature of our souls, and the nature of this life. The only way through life is through it."

I heard a song coming from the juke box. It was one of those songs that describe a hard time as rain coming down on your life. "Hear that?" I said, pointing to the juke box. "Songs say the difficult stuff is like rain. But look at the new life that comes from both."

Sam, still looking over at the juke box, sighed, "Yeah, yeah, I suppose."

"Sam, again, my story is mine."

Sam closed his eyes. "And mine is mine."

I let out a long, deep breath, focusing on what I was about to say. "Once I accepted all that about the hard things in life, things shifted for me. I began to notice that my *resistance* to life, as it really was, began to diminish. I was finally able to stop fighting with life, stop fighting with myself and beating myself up over the stupid things I've done. I could stop saying, 'That shouldn't have happened,' or 'What the hell was I doing?' or 'You idiot!' And I never really noticed how *exhausting* all of that was until I began to stop. You know that feeling when you're bone tired, and you just lie back, let yourself be tired, and let life be what it is?"

"Yeah, like to hell with it all!" Sam nodded.

"Yes! We've all been there. It's not giving up, though. I've come to see it as more of a giving way. It's giving way to where the flow of the Oneness, the Universe, wants to take you. I've found that I could then at least take a step or two toward shifting my focus to 'What's in this *for* me? What can I learn from this?'

"And I know that sounds trite, like I'm Pollyanna. I even feel silly saying it to you, considering all you've been through. I don't mean to diminish anything you've experienced or felt. Actually it's just the opposite. Hell, a pastor friend of mine calls them AFGOs—Another F—n' Growth Opportunity! I love that because it's honest and true. That's what they often feel like."

Sam laughed. "Now *that* resonates with me!"

"What I'm trying to say is that asking the question, 'What's in this for me to learn?' is often the only way we *will* learn. Well, no. I think the things we experience are working on us and changing us even when we have no idea that's going on. I guess what I mean is, by *intentionally* asking the question, we open ourselves up to seeing the difference that the experience makes, so we can move forward."

Sam sat quietly, taking that in.

"Sam, I've discovered that there is power in intention, but we can't intentionally ask that question until we've gone through the worst of the pain. Until then it's not fair of us to expect that of ourselves or of anyone else. When we're hurting so much, we can't come close to the question about what we can learn. For the time being, Sam, I just hope you love yourself."

Sam looked at me as if to say, "How do I do that?"

I thought for a moment. "Sam, once when I was beating myself up over something, I stopped to consider, what would I want a friend to say to me right now? Would I want them to beat me up too? Tell me what an idiot I am? Of course not. I'd want them to still accept me, listen to me, care for me. The Buddhist monk and teacher, Thich Nhat Hanh, has helped me so much with this. He writes about imagining yourself tenderly holding your pain, as a loving parent would hold their child, and say to your pain, 'I'm here for you.' Listen, and tenderly hold your pain. Let it be.

"That may sound crazy and hard to do. But when people are far enough along, I've seen them come to the point where they can ask the question, 'What have I learned?' And the answer sometimes surprises them. You said that you learned that you can be awfully foolish, as you put it. Can you see anything else you've learned?"

Sam thought about it for a while, and then I could tell that a new thought had hit him. "Hmm, I never thought of this before, but I think maybe I was trying to find my way back to love."

"Oh my. What an insight, Sam! I've seen a whole lot of people do a whole lot of things that weren't really the best courses of action. Including me! But it is much more helpful to see *everything* we do as a cry for love—or, as you say, trying to find our way back to love. And that means back to the Love we came from, the Love we still are."

I looked over at Sue who was listening kindly to a woman at the bar. Turning back to Sam, I touched his arm. "I can see the love and light within you, Sam. I see the love you have for Ben and Avery—and even the love you still have for Jadyn. I see the love you have for your students and your colleagues. I see the light that you shine on them."

I looked around at the bar. Sam took a drink and eventually looked up at me.

"Sam, the circumstance you find yourself in now is calling out to you—for you to see what it is offering you. It's all working for us, Sam, all of it. The pain is our driver. It's driving us home to our true Self, where we can remember. If your true self weren't rooted in Love, you wouldn't be so bothered by what you've done. There is an innate knowing within your soul that there is something much, much better within you."

Looking out at the intersection where Ole's Tavern was located, I switched gears a bit. "We all go on our zig-zag way, Sam."

"Yeah, I suppose. Wait, what?"

"When I was a kid, our house was about five blocks away from my school, Garfield Elementary. I loved it there. Everything was the same, year to year—the same school, the same kids in my class. And I walked the exact same way to Garfield every day. I took a left out of our alley, walked a half block to Martini's grocery store on the corner, went right for a block, took a left for one block, then a right for one block. Finally, I took a left and walked one block to Garfield. My family called it my 'zig-zag way.'

"Eventually, I left for college, and my path wasn't set any more. I had to find my own way, but I really didn't know how. When I got to college, I didn't handle my newfound freedom very well, and I did the stupid stuff that many kids do, like drinking—with a few other mistakes added in. But now I don't regret any of it. I needed to do all of those things to grow, to realize that there is a better way to go.

"Sam, I don't believe that the questionable decisions we make are about zigging where we *should* have zagged, or zagging where we *should* have zigged. No, I believe that we are given the freedom to zig and zag when we need to, for the sake of our soul's evolution. I don't judge you for anything, Sam. You've taken every turn you needed to take, your whole life, trying to find your way—just as we all do."

I looked over to the bar, where Sue seemed to be in consolation mode with the woman—being the Presence with her. "Please know, Sam, you come from Love and you are Love. You are one with all that is. At every intersection, in every choice, in every turn, you are never alone."

After a pause, I looked over to the old juke box. "With God, and with this life, I think it's like Robert Polanski, me, and my dad."

Sam looked up from his beer. "What?"

"Have you got time for another when-I-was-a-kid story?"

"Sure."

"There was a bully in our class named Robert Polanski. In fifth grade, Robert walked up to me one day on the playground and told me to give him a nickel the next day or he'd beat me up. Robert was a big kid. Me? Not so much. So the next day I gave him a nickel. Robert figured he had a good thing going, so he kept up with it—plus he upped his price to a quarter. This went on for weeks, and I had to figure out how to keep up. I started sneaking into my dad's change drawer in their bedroom. I felt awful, scared, ashamed.

"One night, my dad came to tuck me in, and he said to me, 'Anything you want to tell me, son?' The dam burst. Through tears, I told him what was going on. I remember my dad hugging me and saying, 'This must have been so hard for you.' He could see that I knew that what I was doing was wrong.

"Then he told me what he wanted me to do the next day. When Robert put out his hand, Dad wanted me to say, 'I'm not giving it to you anymore.'

"Needless to say, I didn't sleep very well that night. The next morning, when the moment of truth came, I told Robert that I wasn't going to give him the quarter and waited for the punch. But the only thing he did was stomp his foot in a puddle I was standing in, and then he walked off.

I laughed. "I remember thinking, 'I went through all this for *that?*'"

"That night, my dad asked me what I'd learned. I learned to stand up for myself. What my dad showed me is how I see God. No judgment—just, 'What did you learn?' It's just like the life review on the other side."

I looked over at a couple in the bar who I know are parents. "It was when I had kids of my own that I felt like I finally knew what my dad and mom must have been feeling that day, waiting to see how the situation would turn out. Man, it's tough being a parent sometimes, isn't it?"

———

Sam looked over at the pool table for a while before he said, "I'd like to meet again, Tim. In fact, I'd like to meet as often as you are willing—while it's summer and easier, at least for me. But next week's really full." Looking at his phone, he said, "I do have Thursday morning open."

"Okay, on Thursday morning I'm meeting with a pastor friend of mine at her church. Are you willing to meet me there after my meeting? We could talk there."

"All right. It will be good to see you in your native habitat, Tim!"

"Ha! See you around ten?"

"Perfect."

When we got out to our cars, I said to Sam, "Your remembering assignment for next time is to love yourself—do something kind for yourself, for your soul."

"All right. See you Thursday morning, my friend!"

8

In the Sanctuary:
Why Things Go Wrong

AFTER PASTOR AMY AND I finished our meeting, I came out of her office and found Sam waiting for me. I introduced Sam and Amy to each other. I said to Sam, "Amy is a wonderful pastor. I just hope the people in this church know how lucky they are."

We had about an hour before Sam had to go. Not wanting to waste any of it driving somewhere, I suggested to Sam that we go into the sanctuary, knowing it would be quiet and private.

When we got inside, I asked Sam to sit with me in the back pew. "This is where Lutherans love to sit. We're a people who seem to have this inborn desire to sit in the back of any room." I pointed to the two chairs up near the altar where pastors sit and said, "It gets lonely sitting up there."

I thought about how I used to look out at the pews and see stories—people's pain as well as their joys. "Sam, the remembering assignment was to love yourself and do something kind for your soul. Did you?"

"I did, but I noticed how resistant I was. It was like part of me was saying that I didn't deserve it, especially after what we talked about the last time we were together."

I looked up at the window above the altar. "Sam, have you ever just sat and let God love you?"

"What do you mean?"

"See that light coming through that window? Imagine that light as the love of God coming toward you in constant, never-ending streams of love. Let's give it a shot, Sam. Just take it in."

So there we were. Two guys sitting where Lutherans feel the most comfortable. The back pew. At times feeling uncomfortable, as the light of love streamed down on the parts of ourselves that we think of as unlovable.

After a few minutes, Sam said, "It's tough to just sit and receive. We're not taught to do that. But *that's* the reality we live in."

"Constantly," I said, never taking my eyes off the window.

Sam looked around the sanctuary. "You said at the workshop that you don't believe that Jesus ever intended to start a new religion."

I shook my head. "Makes no sense to me that he would. When you start a religion, you automatically have some people in the circle and some people outside of it. The people in the circle start thinking that they are right and that the people outside the circle are wrong. Then you have people thinking they've got to get everyone into their circle, or religion, for there to be oneness—when Oneness already exists! It seems to me a religion goes against the Oneness that Jesus taught and lived.

"And there wasn't anything in his message that was religion-friendly. He wasn't teaching any doctrine or correct religious practice. He was talking about a way of *living*, a way of living from the Oneness of all that is, a way of *being*."

"To me, Tim, he never seemed like someone who would want a religion so focused on *him*, as Christianity is—you know, worshiping him and all that."

"I agree, Sam! He would never serve his ego that way. He was never about himself. He was all about God. The Oneness. Jesus does talk about believing in him in the gospels, but the Aramaic scholar I mentioned before, Dr. Neil Douglas-Klotz, told me that the Aramaic word for 'in' can either mean 'in' or 'like.' So instead of 'Believe in me,' we can understand it as 'Believe *like* me. Have the same trust in God that I do. Trust that what I'm teaching you is authentic and trustworthy.' Considering everything else about him, 'Believe *like* me' is the one that makes sense."

I looked around at the pews. "Believing things about someone else only goes so far. Believing things about someone else doesn't invoke the inner transformation that he so wanted for everyone." I turned to Sam, looked him in the eye, and said, "What Jesus cared about was *what you believe about yourself, everyone, and everything around you. That's* what makes the difference in how we live.

"There's a wonderful series of books by Gina Lake, in which she channels Jesus. In *What Jesus Wants You to Know Today*, Jesus says, 'The truth I represent . . . is the truth of your own divine nature, for that is what you are experiencing when you experience me.' He desires to help us remember our true Self. It's our true Self that is drawn to him."

I reached for my wallet and took out a well-worn piece of paper. "Our daughter, Sarah, wrote this. Mind if I read it?"

"Please do."

Within me is an inner cathedral. An enormous, stunning, intricate cathedral. Where wisdom, truth, tranquility, confidence, and spirituality are palpable. A structure built by God and millions of souls. A place that I am still exploring and understanding. A place that is still unfolding itself to me. A place where I bring my life lessons and questions, and they are nurtured and evolve. A space of infinite resources. I cannot access it all the time, but it is always there. I can access it through stillness, poetry, and music; through connecting with others . . . and it is mine. It is built on values so precisely Sarah.

We sat together in the silence . . .

"Oh my, Tim. That's beautiful! Your daughter wrote that?"

"Yep. She did. 'Values so precisely Sarah.'" I added, "I think Sarah does a better job of being Sarah than anyone I know. That's what we're here to do. Be ourselves."

———————

Sam looked up at the cross hanging on the front wall and changed the subject. "You know, I've never believed that whole thing about Jesus dying on a cross so God could forgive us. It seems so gross to me."

"What do you mean?"

"Well, what does that say about God? What kind of a god would require such a horrible thing in order to forgive? We're supposed to think that kind of god is loving? How small, vindictive, and self-absorbed would that god have to be to need *that?*"

I turned to Sam and smiled. "I applaud the trust you have in your inner knowing. You probably just made history, Sam. I doubt that anyone has ever said that before in this space."

"Maybe no one's said it, but I sure used to sit in church and think it!"

"Me too, Sam. But I have no doubt that God is still present in the Church. How could Oneness have it any other way? The One can use Christianity and all the other religions, to do its work. Baptism. Communion. The Bible. The Quran. Sufism. The Tao. Zen Buddhism. God can use all of it. It all can bring great comfort. People's faith and relationship with God is nurtured. I've seen it over and over.

"After I read all the books and visited the communities I told you about, I remember thinking, 'Wow! We Christians limit ourselves to the Bible? There's so much else out there that can help, can give us an expanded, fresh look at things. Open the window. Let in some fresh air!'"

―――――

Sam went on to talk about something else he never understood when he was in church. "The Trinity! The Father, Son, and Holy Spirit. Three in one. What the heck is that about?"

I shook my head, "That's okay, Sam. None of the men who came up with that idea knew what it was all about either! And I emphasize the word *men*. One woman told me it sounded like a dysfunctional family. "'Where's the mother?' she said.

"And I never saw it make any difference in how people live. It was like those three were over there somewhere, doing their thing. But what does that have to do with us?" I looked out the window and saw a car driving by. "We had Trinity Sunday every year, and I could never imagine anyone driving to church that day, thinking, 'Wow! Trinity Sunday today! I can't wait!'"

"The trinity that does make all the difference in how we live, the one that resonates with me, is what I call the *trinity of Oneness*. I think that's what Jesus was talking about when he said everything can be summed up in this: 'Love God, and your neighbor, as yourself.' It's about knowing that any time we are loving any *one* of them, we are loving the *other two* as well. When we love God, we love our neighbor and ourselves, for God is within our neighbor and ourselves. When we love our neighbor or ourselves, we love God, for God is within our neighbor and ourselves."

"What flows within all three is Divine Love. Hmm. The trinity of Oneness. I like that," Sam said.

"There's a reason you do."

I looked around at the empty pews. "We never told them, Sam." Tears welled up in my eyes as I turned to Sam and said what I believe is the greatest failure of the Christian Church. "We never told them what they are! We told them that *God* is love. We told them that *Jesus* loves them. We told them that they *should* love. But we never told them *they* are Divine Love at their core," I said, sweeping my hand across the pews.

"Instead, we told them they are the opposite. We said that they are sinners, that their very nature is 'sinful and unclean,' to use the words of a confession that I used to lead at the start of every service. Do we do unloving things that are called sins? Of course! Do we hurt those around us? Of course! But we do those things because we forget our true nature, which is Oneness and love, not because that *is* our nature."

I laughed. "When our daughter, Sarah, was young, she had a dear friend, Mari. They were inseparable! One day as they were playing, Mari said, 'Oh! I forgot to remember!' I just love that. We forget to remember what we truly are, because of something we all have as humans—an ego."

Sam nodded his head, "As in being egotistical, self-centered."

"Yeah, that's the way we normally think of it. But you're not a bad person if you have an ego. Everyone has an ego. I call it standard-issue equipment when our soul incarnates as a human. It serves its purposes here. We need confidence in ourselves to accomplish what our soul came here to do. Plus, the ego actually serves us spiritually."

"How so?"

"When our soul incarnates, it agrees to marry an ego. It's a marriage of two very different energies living together. There is the soul, our true Self, which emerges out of the One. It is beautiful and is here to grow into its potential of love and wisdom. Our soul knows, at some level, that its identity and security are found only in its Oneness with its Source. It is cherished beyond description by its Source, and we are here to learn to love and cherish ourselves as well.

"The other partner in the marriage is an ego that sees itself and everything else as separate. This sense of separation produces one major emotion: fear. Of course the ego is afraid, since it thinks it's on its own. So it's always looking for what it thinks it needs, that is, to be in control. And the ego is always looking for more—more approval, more accomplishments, more recognition, a more impressive title. It loves comparing itself to others and coming out on top, because, with its fearful sense of separateness and aloneness, it has an insatiable craving to build itself up.

"Those two opposing energies create a problem for the marriage. There's tension within the home, the home of us. There's angst, confusion, insecurity, anxiety. These are all fear-based. When we judge others, we do it out of fear. When we act in harmful ways out of anger, we are afraid. When we lie, we're afraid. When we worry or are anxious, we're afraid. When we feel out of control, we're afraid. When things inevitably change and we resist that change, we're afraid. When we show prejudice, we're afraid."

Sam jumped in, "Hmm, I judge out of fear. I never traced my judging back to fear before."

"Sam, the things that the Church and Christianity label as sins are all fueled by fear. They're all sure signs of living from the ego that sees itself as separate, and not from our soul, our true Self, that knows better. But you're not a failure as a spiritual person if you're afraid. Fear is part of the human experience. Fear comes to you as everything else does in this world. It comes as a teacher."

I turned to Sam. "Here's the thing with the ego. It's not real. The ego is only an empty illusion, like darkness. Darkness seems so real to us, but it's not a thing unto itself. It's actually the absence of something—the absence of light. If we were here at night, and we turned on the light . . ."

Sam nodded. "We'd see the darkness for what it really is. Nothing."

"Exactly. And the ego is also the *absence of the awareness of Oneness*. It's an illusion of separation, because there never has been any separation from God, from each other, or from our true Self. Separation is impossible, but the pain our egos can provide has its ironic purpose. Knowing a deep sadness stretches us to receive a deeper joy. Hopelessness creates an expanded space to welcome an enduring hope. Worry and fear allow us to receive the depths of a true peace. Knowing a sense of separation allows us to welcome true connection and Oneness. It's all working together as One."

I paused to think about my own experiences with such things and then continued. "Sam, that's all to say that we are *not* sinful by nature. We do fear-based, harmful things because we're lost in the illusions of the ego that sees us as separate. Eventually, we grow weary of the pain and emptiness of living with the energy of our fearful and needy ego. We leave the marriage, so to speak, and return home to our true Self, rooted in the One's love. That's the spiritual work we're here to do."

———————

After a pause, I looked out over the pews. "Anyway. We rarely told them about the cathedral that they are, having the presence of God inside them. When we occasionally did, it seemed to me that people didn't know what to do with that truth or couldn't really believe it—not after being pounded over the head for so many years about being sinners."

Sam looked out the window. "You know, people are always talking about *going to* church where God is, when in fact they're already there, all the time."

"Oh, tell me more!"

"Well, if that inner cathedral stuff is really true—and I believe it is—then everyone comes here bringing the presence of God within them. Their own cathedral, as Sarah would say."

"Oh! Preach it, brother! With that in mind, did you know the number one reason people go to church?"

"I would guess it has to do with the people they know here."

"Exactly, community—they come for the community, for connection. And I believe that, whether they realize it or not, what they're ultimately looking for in each other is God—a return to their common Source."

I noticed Sam looking toward the front. "Look at the set-up here, Sam. Everything is facing forward, as if all the action is up there at the altar. This layout is saying 'That's where God is!' People should actually be *facing each other* instead of sitting with their backs to each other. They should be affirming and entering into each other's cathedrals."

"How do you do that?" Sam asked.

"I believe that singing, listening, sharing, praying, laughing, loving are all experienced in a fuller way by facing each other. But we're always thinking about what we're going to do. We want to fill up the space and the silence, when in fact it is already filled. We're entering into the presence of God, just being—being together, sharing space and time.

"I attended a Quaker meeting where we sat in silence for nearly an hour. Afterward we stood up and greeted one another. I've never felt so connected to a group of people I hadn't known. We met in the silence, and it was fascinating."

Looking out over the empty pews, I said, "I often wonder what would have happened if we had told them what they truly are, if we had helped them remember."

———————

"Have you ever wondered why Avery was born with Down syndrome?"

"About a thousand times, especially just after she was born."

"Have you ever thought of your divorce as nothing but a failure?"

"Sometimes it's easy for me to go there. How could I not? It didn't exactly end as a rousing success!"

"Several years ago, Sam, I began to learn about what is called prebirth planning, and things started to make a whole lot more sense to me. Prebirth planning happens on the other side before our soul incarnates in this lifetime. Our soul comes together with elders and other souls, and a basic plan for our lives is designed. It's the plan that best offers the experiences that our soul or other souls need at that particular point in their evolution. Older souls, because of their experiences in many lives, are allowed more input into the circumstances of their upcoming lives than younger souls. Even so, a lot is left wide open to the choices we make here, because God is Love, and Love never forces itself on anyone. The Oneness gives and honors free will."

"So there's this basic structure or architecture to our lives that is preplanned?"

"Architecture is a good word for it, Sam. The major structures that influence our life experiences are preplanned. Like the family we are born into, because our family has such a huge impact on us. Souls agree to play roles in the drama that we associate with family life. One agrees to be the wife, another the husband. One might be the partner, the father, the mother, the sister. Others agree to be significant friends and so on. These roles may all be different in another life.

"You described the first time you held your children at birth. That was so beautiful. You said you didn't know where that feeling of 'I know you' came from. I believe it came from your remembering just a bit about those earlier agreements. Your children's souls agreed to be your children in this life, and you agreed to be their father. To say your souls go way back is an epic understatement."

Sam turned to me. "You know, what I felt matches up with what you just said."

"Fascinating, isn't it?" I continued, "All these souls are at their own levels of development, and they all need to grow. That really makes sense to me, as I look back on those families I knew as a pastor. As I see it now, *no family is perfect, but they were all perfect for each other* in providing the drama, angst, and joys that their souls needed at that particular point to potentially grow and learn from each other. We need to remember that a human family is actually a group of *souls* coming together as humans. I say 'potentially grow and learn,' because it's up to us, Sam. We can come here and not learn a damn thing."

Scanning the pews, I remembered families I knew, and where they always sat in the sanctuary. "Sam, you said you grew up in a dysfunctional family. Did you ever hear someone say they grew up in a functional family? But actually, yours was functional in its own way—dysfunctionally functional, you might say."

I noticed the differences in our bodies. Sam still looked strong and athletic. My body still has its slim build. "Another thing that is often chosen is the *body* we are born into. Our bodies provide so much experience unique to our soul's needs. It makes a lot of sense to me now that I have lived in a skinny body, in this life as Tim Tengblad. I've been told that I've had other lives in which I was very athletic and strong, so that explains part of why it's been such a challenge for me.

"More importantly, that experience lifted up great compassion and empathy, already within me, for anyone who is made to feel less than or left out. I knew something of what that felt like and was drawn to people who were experiencing being left out. That was a big part of my ministry. I now see that this body that I resisted for so long was actually helping me to get to know my true Self. Everything was working together as One."

"So what about Avery?"

"Oh, dear Avery. Of course I can't sit here and say that I know, but it makes sense to me that Avery's soul may have needed or chose to come here with Down syndrome. There was either something that *she* needed to learn through that experience, or there were things that you, Jadyn, and Ben needed to learn from her, as her family. That's why you all signed up. So for purposes of the soul, there is actually love, instead of just sadness, in her having Down syndrome. From the human perspective, that is hard to see and accept."

"Love and a whole lot of courage."

"Oh my goodness. Souls are so courageous!"

I heard people talking behind us in the atrium. "I loved hearing you talk about how Avery loves and connects with people."

"Avery does show the world great things."

"Sam, I have a friend whose grandson has a disability. She says, 'He loves me into being.' I love that."

"I love that too," Sam said, as he looked out a nearby window. "I'm just trying to realize why that feels so good." After a moment, he turned to me. "You talk about our souls coming from the One-ness. To me that sounds like we are pure being at our core, before we think, say, or do anything. Maybe that's why, if we can stop our doing and just be, it feels so good, so peaceful, so right."

"Hmm. There's some good stuff there, Sam. Let me just be with that thought."

After a minute, Sam broke the silence. "You're saying that Jadyn and I agreed to be husband and wife?" Sam lamented.

"I think so, Sam. When we first met at Ole's, you said that you knew the moment you met Jadyn that you were going to get married. Where do you think that came from?"

Sam looked up at the choir loft to our right. "Interesting question. Yeah, maybe it came from prebirth planning. But look at how it turned out!"

"Sam, it resonates with me that maybe you and Jadyn made a contract with each other to be in each other's lives for the length of time you were together, to provide each other the experiences you both needed. Maybe you learned all that you were supposed to learn in that marriage, or maybe you needed to experience what divorce taught you at this point in your growth and evolution. Maybe what happened simply came out of choices that you made through your free will, and it all could have gone another way. In any case, I believe that there is purpose and meaning behind it all."

"Yeah, but I still don't see why anyone in their right mind would *choose* any of this? You'd have to be some kind of a masochist."

"Good point, Sam! I know it sounds crazy on *this* side. It doesn't sound rational to us when we are human. I think it's because we're not *in* our human minds when we make those choices before birth.

"I've come to learn that, on the other side, there is a greater knowing of ourselves as souls and our eternal nature. Living in that awareness, our souls are much more courageous. It's kind of like, 'Okay. Let's take on this hard thing. Why not?'"

"Hmm. That really changes the whole question of 'Why did God do this to me?'"

"It did for me, Sam."

"So, it's not God in a distant heaven pushing buttons and creating hard things for us."

"No, just the opposite. God is perfect Love. *We* are in on the creation of our story, both on the other side and here. We are co-creators of our soul's story, along with the Oneness."

Sam looked at the empty pews. "So the preplanning is something that we and spirit collaborate on. And how it all turns out is also a matter of our choices and spirit's influence."

"You got it, I believe."

Sam looked out the window for a bit. "I have a teacher friend whose wife died of cancer at age thirty-five, leaving two kids. He told me he stopped going to church because he was pissed at God, because God did that to his wife or did nothing to stop it."

"I get it. If that's what you believe, of course you're going to get angry and say, 'To hell with it.' I've had my own struggles with that in the past. It seems so unfair to us when someone dies young. We decide that someone died before their time. Maybe so. But it made sense to me when I learned that some souls come here to live a relatively short life in a particular lifetime. Maybe it's for their own growth or maybe to provide an experience that the souls of their family members needed for their growth. Maybe it propelled them toward what they could become and do in that lifetime."

"I don't know much, Tim, but it sure seems like there's a whole lot more going on than we know about on this side."

"I don't know much either, Sam, but I do believe we're cocreators of our soul's story, both on the other side before we come here and while we're here. A whole mysterious plan and process are being worked out, and underneath it all there is Love driving the story, even when the opposite of Love seems to be happening. Everything is for our souls' growth into the Love we came from and naturally are.

"I've also learned that we remember all this when we are back on the other side. The contracts, as they are called, that we made with one another before we came here are remembered. There is opportunity to reflect, process, learn, and continue growing on the other side."

Sam looked out the window again. "Wow. So fascinating. I'll have to think about all of this."

––––––––––––

We both noticed the time. We stood up and left the sanctuary. When we got out to our cars, I looked back at the sanctuary and laughed. "I sounded like I know so much. I used to do that a lot in there. I see only shadows in this world, Sam—glimmers from my soul—while a lot remains mystery. I've got to say, I'm glad it is mystery. That makes it all so fascinating. It tells me that the truth is so magnificent that it takes lifetimes and beyond."

As we were getting into our cars, Sam yelled over, "I play golf, you know! Not very well, but I play. How about we meet next time on the golf course? Next Tuesday?"

"You're playing my song, Sam! I'll make a tee time at my favorite course and let you know. Oh—your remembering assignment for next time is to think about people who have inspired you."

"Got it!"

Part 3

9

On the Golf Course: Living and Learning

OUR START TIME ON THE golf course was 9:05 a.m. It was a cool morning with a chance of rain later on. Before we started playing, we spent some time together on the practice range, loosening up by hitting some practice balls.

I asked Sam about the remembering assignment I'd given him of thinking about people who have inspired him. He said, "I thought about a physics teacher I had in high school. She was amazing! Her love for physics and her students just drew me in. I wasn't the only one who became a physics teacher because of her."

After I hit a ball, I turned to Sam. "I asked you to do that because it's my experience that when we are inspired by someone, we are being *in-spirited*. What we admire in someone else is actually within us as well, otherwise we wouldn't be so attracted to them. What is already within us is being stirred and wants to come out and play. When we want to be like someone, there is a reason for that. We are like that person, but in our own way."

After Sam hit another practice ball, I continued. "Sam, coming out of Divine Love, you are the wonder and love that you saw in your teacher. I'm sure you're a very good teacher. I can see it in your eyes. I can feel it in your energy. I hope your students know that. Most of them probably don't at this age, but I have no doubt that someday they'll look back, remember, and see what they had."

"Thanks, Tim. I try to be." After almost completely missing the ball, he laughed. "Hope I'm better at being a teacher than I am at this golf thing!"

After we walked to the first tee, I said to Sam, "This place helps me remember. Hope abounds before the first shot. Hit away, Sam!"

Sam swung and his ball took off to the right, into some trees. I got up and hit one into the trees on the left.

I let out a "*Scheisse!*" as we walked off the tee. "I learned that word from a pastor friend of mine I used to play golf with, who spoke fluent German. It's a good word—comes in handy, especially out here!"

Sam laughed as we parted ways. "I don't know German, but I think I've got a handle on that one."

"Like I said at the tavern, people get so weird out here when they find out I was a pastor. I get the 'Oh! I'm going to have to watch my language' bit. But now I just say, 'Go ahead and say whatever you want. I really don't give a shit what you say.' Then we laugh, and from that point on we're just people playing golf."

Sam stopped walking and said. "But why is it so hard to hit a golf ball, Tim? I mean the ball is just sitting there. It's not coming at you ninety-five miles an hour, like a baseball."

I shook my head, "Ha! And why do we play it? If you want to learn humility, Sam, play golf. Or work in a church."

"Or teach!" Sam yelled over to me. "Or parent!"

"Or be human!" I shouted back.

We hit our next shots, and as we walked closer together I said, "Golf, life, being human can all be so hard. And we all know, no matter what we do, that no one ever masters any of them. It's my experience that they're supposed to be hard until we learn not to make them so hard. We create a lot of our own suffering with all three."

After we finished the first hole, Sam asked me on the way to the next hole, "Okay. What did you mean by learning not to make golf and life so hard? I'd like to sign up for that."

"I think what works with golf, Sam, carries over to life and being human. The most important thing is not to get in your own way. Just watch people out here. They stand over the ball much too long. And you know they're thinking about five different things with their swing. The great golf pro from years ago, Sam Snead, said, 'Analysis is paralysis.' That works for a lot of things. Once you're over the ball, just swing already!"

We hit our drives on the second hole, and Sam seemed to swing even harder this time, causing the ball to go high and even farther right, into the trees. I swung easier this time, and the ball went perfectly straight.

Sam hit his ball back out of the woods, toward my ball. As we walked together, I asked him, "When you were hitting back there, what were you trying to do?"

Sam shrugged his shoulders and said, "I was trying to hit it straight, where your ball is."

I followed with, "And I noticed you swung harder than you had before. Was there a reason for that?"

"Yeah," Sam said, "the first shot I hit today didn't go very far and went to the right. So I was trying to hit it farther and steer it there too."

"I've done that a million times myself. Did you succeed?" I asked.

Sam shook his head. "It only went farther to the right."

I started laughing. "I was just thinking about a verse from Romans Seven in the New Testament. Paul says,

> *I do not understand my own actions.*
> *For I do not do what I want, but I do the very thing I hate.*

"I know he wasn't talking golf there, but it sure sounds like it! He was talking about the inner battle going on within him and us all. He didn't use these words, but I see him talking about the inner battle of our ego with our true Self—our true Self being what we are in God, and what God is in us. We've all got this part of us that wants to do good, and another part of us, the ego, that wants to control and manipulate everything according to its needs."

By this time we were at my ball. We had to wait for the group ahead of us, so I continued. "Sam, back there, would you say you were swinging from fear?"

"Yeah, I was. I was afraid I wouldn't do what I want, but instead do the very thing I was trying not to do! But how do you *not* do that?"

"Sam, whenever we do anything out of fear or insecurity, it's a sure sign we're swinging or living from the ego. The ego is always afraid and insecure, because it feels like it lacks something. So it is constantly trying to control and manipulate."

I took a club out of my bag and swung it back to the top of my backswing.

"It's right here, Sam, where I can feel my ego kicking in. I'm all loaded up here at the top of my swing. I look down at the ball, and I just want to hit it hard and control where it goes. I swing too hard and actually lose control. Men have a particularly hard time not over-swinging. We want to grip it and rip it, as guys like to say. But if I check my ego as I swing, if I relax, take it back slower, slow my downswing, and let go of trying to control the ball, it has a much greater chance of going where I want it to go."

As we walked toward the next shot, Sam said, "So the way to go is to swing from love and not fear?"

"Swing from love! I like that, Sam! Which is to live from your true Self. Your true Self naturally trusts the flow."

As we were walking, I said to Sam, "If you watch people swing out here, most are trying to help the club do its job." We watched someone hit a shot. "See how they tried to help the club get the ball up? The club is *made* to get the ball in the air. It doesn't need our help. It just needs us to get out of its way and let it do what it's designed to do. It's the same with the Oneness. We're already in it. Oneness just needs us to get out of its way, so it can naturally do what it wants to do."

As we walked toward the green, I noticed Sam was watching a woman hitting her ball with a beautiful, even-tempo, graceful swing. He shouted over to me, "Now there's someone not swinging from their ego!"

On the green, Sam got over his ball and quickly stroked a nice, long putt ending up about a foot from the cup. "Nice putt, Sam!"

After we finished the hole, I turned to Sam. "If I think too much out here, I can't do anything to save my soul."

We walked over to the third hole and had to wait for the group ahead of us to finish. I walked over to Sam. "Speaking of saving souls," I said shaking my head. "The Church and Christianity have spent so much of their history trying to *save* souls. Which implies saving souls from being sent to hell. Which implies saving souls from God, if you think about it. Who else is going to send you to hell besides God? That's a ludicrous thing to hang over people's heads. Love would *never* create such a place. A God of Love sending people to eternal torture? Give me a break! We create our own hells, Sam—hells that are always rooted in fear, caused by a false sense of separation from our Source."

"But where *did* that whole hell thing come from?" Sam asked, as he sat on the bench beside the tee.

"Here's the short answer. It's mostly about power, control, and the male ego. Until very recently, it was all men running the show, and still is in many churches. Think about it, Sam. The Church creates this place of eternal punishment and suffering. Then the Church tells people that only the Church can give them what they need so they don't go to hell. The Church says, 'Keep coming to us, give us money, confess your sins, believe what we tell you, and then we will offer God's forgiveness.' So it's human power and control, *and* humans have a long history of attributing to God how *they themselves* operate. If we were honest, most of us want people to feel guilty and suffer some consequences for the stuff they do to us. We call it justice."

I sat down on the bench next to Sam. "Souls don't need to be saved from hell or God. They only need to be saved from the hell that our own ego creates from its fears and insecurities. Then souls can flourish and grow. They need to be saved from our getting in our own way. They need to be honored by listening to them."

I looked straight ahead at the group in front of us. "The Divine essence of the soul doesn't know insecurity, because it is secure in its Source. It doesn't know inferiority, so it has no need to feel superior. When we get in touch with that, when we remember, *then* golf, life, and being human become, well, not as hard as we make it. *That* is when we start swinging and living from love."

As the group ahead finished, I stood up. "The irony is, it's the human ego's fears and insecurities that cause the growth of the soul. We have to live them until we learn from them. Ha! Your profession mirrors life, Sam! Everything comes as teacher—everything. Ah, the lesson plans that the ego brings! We have to live and learn from the ego and its fears, until we see it all for what it is. An endless dead end."

After we hit our shots, Sam said, "I get what you're saying, but there are a lot of moving parts in the golf swing. Isn't it good to learn how all that can fit together?"

"Sure. I think taking lessons can be a good start to build a foundation. It's important to learn about a proper grip of the club, stance, body posture, balance, how to take the club back properly, how to start the downswing with the hips, all of that. But you can't stand over the ball and swing thinking about all of that. Snead was right: 'Analysis is paralysis!' That's where practice comes in. In practice, in repeating proper swings, you build up muscle and timing memory in the body. Eventually you'll get to the point where you can actually feel that the body knows what to do, without thinking about anything."

Sam hit his second shot pretty well. "I felt like I just let my body do what it wanted to do that time."

"With the soul," I continued, "I've found it's actually easier. While you have to build up muscle memory in the body, the soul already has a built-in memory. It has a knowing of what it is, because it innately knows what it came from. It *is* what it came from. The essence of your soul already knows love, peace, hope, compassion, meaning, and purpose, because it emerged from all of that."

As we walked, I asked Sam, "Ever wonder why you're doing this seeking that you're doing?"

"It's because I want more of what you just mentioned in my life. Don't we all?"

"And *why* do you want it, Sam? Could it be because there is something within you that already is those things? And that something just wants to be known, grown into, and remembered?'"

"Interesting. So it's like, why would you seek after love, peace, or happiness if you don't know anything about them?"

I smiled. "Exactly!"

"Yeah. That resonates with me."

"So, Sam, in golf and in life, practice and let the remembering naturally happen. Just as you practice golf swings to build up muscle and timing memory in your body, practice remembering what your soul already knows. Do the things that stimulate what the soul knows, the things that cause that knowing to rise up into your awareness—and live from there. Keep doing the things I'm encouraging you to do in your remembering assignments."

When Sam and I finished the hole, I asked him, "So what can we do to practice remembering what our soul already knows?"

"Well, we've talked about practicing kindness, being in the moment, being part of something bigger than yourself, listening to music, and creating. You know what works for you."

"All of those are called spiritual *practices*, because we probably won't be very good at most of them right away. It takes investing ourselves in them, over and over, until we gradually realize that they are our natural place to live from."

———————

We hit our first shot on the next hole and started walking. "Sam, when I suggest certain things like practicing being present, or not identifying with thoughts in the head, people sometimes come back at me with, 'I tried that. But it's so hard!' I usually say, 'Yeah, it's hard, especially at first. But like with anything else, the reason it's hard is that you've been doing it another way for so long. It takes time to build up a new habit.'"

Sam chimed in. "Yeah, sometimes I want to say to my students, isn't the way you've been doing it hard?"

"Exactly. Isn't it hard to get lost in your spinning mind or stay fixated on the past or spin worrisome stories about a future that hasn't happened and isn't real? We have a choice of which kind of hard we want to live with."

"I always tell my students, that it gets easier the more you work with what we're doing."

As we were finishing the ninth hole, I said, "You know, in golf, it seems like every player has one dominant thing they're working on developing. My dad was always working on not dropping his right shoulder, which made him hit too much of the ground with his club. With me, it's not rushing the down swing. With souls, it's the same thing. Every soul is here to work on something. It might be developing patience, acceptance or empathy, or maybe it's learning to value themselves. What do you think you're here to work on, Sam?"

As we walked over to the next hole, I could tell Sam was thinking about it. "Acceptance, among other things." He laughed. "Well, actually, there's quite a list!"

"I've got my own list too, but, like you, one stands out for me. It's learning to value what my soul knows, to be confident enough in what my soul knows to share that with others."

I stopped walking and turned to Sam. "Being around you encourages me to accept that I've come to be a teacher, just like you. Thanks for that!"

As we made the turn to the last nine holes, I started to laugh. "Remember how I said I like being at Ole's Tavern because they treat me like a normal person?"

"Yeah, I remember that."

"As I said, people would get so weird when they found out I was a pastor. I'd hit a good shot and I'd hear, 'must be the clean living.' Or 'pays to have connections.' All that crap. So I started taking on aliases. I've been an architect, a teacher, a marriage and family therapist. I've been a mortician. That shuts 'em up pretty fast. One time, when I was playing with my friend Jack, I said I was an OB/GYN! Jack couldn't believe I'd said that. When we got back to our cart, he said to me, 'Do you even know what those letters mean?'"

———————

By the time we got to the twelfth hole, the rain that was forecast began to fall.

"What do you think?" I asked Sam. "Want to go in or stay out here?"

Sam looked up and to the west. "Well, it looks like it should let up fairly soon. Let's keep going."

Sam and I hit our tee shots into the wind and rain as if everything we'd been talking about was forgotten. Both of us swung harder and faster.

As we walked along, Sam laughed. "Okay, I know what just happened! When things get harder, the ego wants to double down and try harder to control and manipulate. And I suppose the thing to do is just the opposite. Keep swinging your normal swing, nice and easy. Trust it."

I laughed. "Absolutely! But obviously, I still need some work on practicing what I preach. You know, the thing about an easy swing, one with a smooth tempo, is that you have to trust that there is enough power in it to get the job done. When things get tough, the challenge is to just keep trusting that we have what we need to get through to a nice finish."

After we finished the thirteenth hole, I said, "I like what you said back there about swinging your normal swing. Arnold Palmer always said, 'Swing *your* swing.' He had a very unique swing.

"There are some basics to the game that we all have to pay attention to, but your body is going to want to do things that mine won't. It's the same with your mind. Go for it! And even though our souls are the same in some respects, they're all unique. Our souls experience things differently, and they want to express themselves differently than anyone else's. Go for it! The soul isn't here to live like anyone else."

As we walked toward the fourteenth tee, I continued, "Don't forget you're unique, Sam—just like everybody else."

Sam played holes fourteen and fifteen very well and my game fell apart. Walking toward the sixteenth, I stopped and looked at the last hole we'd just played. "As I think of the thousands of holes I've played, it's all about gratitude. It's about appreciation for just being out here—and less about how I play. That can be one of the gifts of getting older—appreciating just being."

Holes sixteen and seventeen went well for me. My swing felt great. The ball was going where I wanted it to go. Walking off seventeen, Sam commented, "You're in the zone now!"

I just laughed. "Been here a thousand times, Sam. Golf and life are a lot alike that way. Just when you think you're in control, golf and life just laugh at you and show you differently. Out here, just when you think you've found the key, it's like someone changes the locks on you. Then you start looking for a new key.

"I've got a notepad of my dad's that I carry in my golf bag. I treasure it. In it are his dated, handwritten notes about what he was working on each day with his swing. My heart feels connected again, just looking at his handwriting. His notes are all about what he was trying to do with his hips, shoulders, legs, and so on, on that particular day. We're funny. We're always trying to find something perfect in golf and life. The answer remains the same: it's always within, just waiting to be remembered."

"Live and swing from love," Sam observed. "Whatever that means for each of us."

"That's how I see it too."

Our play continued, and sure enough, just when I thought I had it, I played the eighteenth hole horribly. I hit my first shot well into the trees. "*Scheisse!*" I muttered.

After my second "*Scheisse!*" shot, I said, "You know, golf is hard, but it does give you this constant, annoying opportunity to practice letting go of liking or disliking. When you hit a bad shot, the ego's spontaneous response is to not like it, reject it, along with muttering a few *Scheisse*s! The shot doesn't care what you think about it. It's not going to change for you! Neither does anything else that happens in life for that matter. So why beat yourself up? What you learned from that swing, that shot—that's all that matters."

We walked a little further, and I laughed. "Look at me. I just said that, but I still mutter my *Scheisse*s. I played the other day with a woman who was a great player. I told her what I just told you, and she said, 'But I don't *have to* like it, and I'm not going to!' Okay, if you want to keep knocking your head against the wall, go ahead. Knock yourself out! I've done it a million times."

Walking down the eighteenth and last hole, I turned to Sam. "I remember when I started reading from Buddhism. I found that Buddhism has so much to offer in terms of acceptance of what is. It speaks of moving beyond like and dislike, want and don't want, should or shouldn't be happening, and all of that. It's about just seeing everything for what it really is, without our commentary. I've found that to be so freeing. You find it's never as bad as the story you're spinning about it, and life is much less exhausting.

"That's part of what I meant on the first hole about making golf and life harder than it is, about creating a lot of our own suffering.

Oftentimes the reason we suffer so much when something happens is that we decided it should be different than it is. We think that what happened is what makes us suffer, when we're actually creating our own suffering by how we're responding to it."

After we finished the last hole, Sam asked me, "Want to go in for a couple of barley pops?"

"Sure. I never turn that down!"

When we sat down in the bar area, I asked Sam what his takeaway was from today.

"Well, I really like the thing about not forcing the swing—or anything, for that matter."

"Yeah, mine is what you said about swinging from love. I'm taking that one with me! Relaxed, not forcing, just letting it happen. When you've tried to force anything, Sam, how has it gone?"

"Not so well. In fact, it never has, as I look back. It's also exhausting."

"That it is. It seems we all know when we are trying to force something to happen. It just feels awful, and it's a whole lot of work."

"Here's to swinging and living from love!" Sam says as he raised his glass.

"Cheers!"

Looking out the window at the eighteenth hole, I said, "Oh, Sam, you experience it all out there—joy, anger, frustration, fear, confusion, satisfaction, feeling overwhelmed and defeated, accomplishment, feeling the illusion of being in control."

"Tim, you talk a lot about love, and love being our ultimate truth, but there's a whole lot that isn't love in me."

"To be sure, Sam. I love what Rumi wrote, 'Your task is not to seek for love, but merely to seek and find all the barriers within yourself that you have built against it, and embrace them.' It's the *embracing* part that's hard, of course. It's hard to look at the barriers to love that we've created within and learn from them. Once we've embraced and learned, the barriers can start to come down, and the love that is already there within us is free to rise up, and we remember."

"I get it, but that can be tough."

"Well, let me throw it back at you. When you left the house, and your separation and divorce started unfolding, what were you feeling?"

Sam looked down as if he was closing himself off from everyone in the room. "Fear. Fear of the unknown. Fear of being alone. Fear of being away from my kids."

"When you found out about Avery's Down syndrome, what did you feel?"

"To be honest, anger. Especially at first. Fear. I was afraid of how to be a parent to her. I didn't have a clue."

"Have you ever just sat with your fear as if it were sitting across from you in a chair? Ask it questions? If you were to ask your fear what it was so afraid of in those times, what do you think it would say, Sam?"

"I think it would say that it was afraid of pain. With the marriage ending, I think I was afraid that it would all be too painful and overwhelming."

"Was it painful?"

"Hell, yeah!"

"After you felt the pain, Sam, did you find it was as bad as you told yourself it would be? Was it completely overwhelming, or were you able to gradually handle it?"

"It *was* overwhelming at first, but yeah, I eventually realized I could handle it, that it wasn't going to be overwhelming forever."

"Tell me, teacher, what did that teach you?"

"I discovered strength I didn't know I had."

"It was always there. Just waiting to be discovered. Tell me, Sam, as you and Jadyn went along with parenting Avery, did you *really* not have a clue, or did you discover that you did?"

Sam nodded. "With help from our community, we discovered that we did."

"Okay. I'm happy for you both. That's what I mean by being willing to embrace all that we are and experience as humans. At the end of the day, and all during the day, it's good to be human. Of course, that's easier said than done."

"I suppose so. I wish there was an easier way, though," Sam lamented.

"I do too, Sam. Sometimes, I wish *golf* were easier, but then again, the challenge of it is what I love the most. I think our souls look at life the same way. The soul sees life and being human so differently than our egos do. Your soul made the tee time for this game of life, Sam! It's here for experiences. To the soul, life *is* experiences."

We lifted our glasses. "To our souls! Brave they be!"

As we walked out to our cars, I said to Sam, "I've loved being out here with you, Sam. There's a nature preserve close to here. Are you game to meet there next Thursday, say nine a.m.?"

Sam gave a thumbs up. "Sounds good!"

Getting into my car, I yelled over to Sam. "Next remembering assignment: be."

"Be what?"

"Just be. Try sitting and being, not doing anything, not spinning anything in your mind about the past or future. Just be."

10

At the Nature Preserve:
Allowing and Accepting

IN WHAT HAD BECOME OUR ritual, I met Sam in the parking lot, this time at the nature preserve. It was a beautiful morning, with the mist dissipating in the sun, like those thoughts in our minds when we shine the light of our observation on them. As we walked, I thought of a recent visit to Walden Pond, near Concord, Massachusetts.

"Ever been to Walden Pond?" I asked Sam.

"You mean where Henry David Thoreau wrote his book?"

"Yeah, where he wrote *Walden*."

"No, I haven't been there."

"I'd recommend a visit. It's a lovely place. I was just thinking about something he wrote that's on a plaque near the tiny cabin where he lived for two years. He wrote:

*I went to the woods because
I wished to live deliberately,
to front only the essential facts of life, and see if I
could not learn what it had
to teach, and not, when I
come to die, discover that
I had not lived.*

We kept walking as we soaked that one in, and I asked Sam how the remembering assignment of just being went for him.

"Oh, man. That was the hardest of all. The first time I tried to just sit there, I just thought, 'I can't do this.' My mind was going crazy. I got really restless and got up and did something. The second time I lasted a little bit longer. The third time, a little longer. By the fourth time, I started to notice the part of me that really liked just being. I loved the rest and the sense of increasing peace. I just kept taking deep breaths, just noticing my breath going in and out. By the fifth time, it started to feel a bit like I was coming home."

"Wow, Sam. Good for you for sticking with it like that. Yeah, just being is our natural state. We are pure being at our core, because our souls emerged from Oneness, from God. Oneness is pure being itself. God names itself 'I am' in the book of Exodus in the Old Testament. In our pure Being, we don't have to accomplish anything or earn approval or acceptance. We are loved simply because we are. Just being resonates with our core being."

I pointed to a couple of spots that were good for sitting. I suggested that we separate for a bit, so we could, as Thoreau wrote, front only the essential facts of life and see what it had to teach.

After about twenty minutes, I walked over to Sam. "Thoughts?"

Looking out over the preserve, Sam said, "This is God's first cathedral. It was here long before humans came around."

"I love that, Sam. God's first cathedral. Thank you."

"There's only the sound of the birds. It's so peaceful and quiet," Sam observed. "I grow fonder of peace and quiet as I age."

"Me too! Look around you, Sam. Everything is content to be what it is and to allow everything around it to be what it is. There is nothing here trying to be anything other than what it is, nothing trying to be something else. There is little resistance to life as it is."

We sat in the silence.

"Look at that tall, straight tree over there, and that shorter tree that bends to the right next to it. They allow and accept each other and themselves, as they are. There's an evergreen tree over there that's missing half its branches. Nothing out here says it should be any different than it is. There is in nature so much allowing and accepting of *what is*. When it rains, it rains. When the sun shines, it shines. When the wind blows, it blows. The trees that have open space within them allow the storm to be what it is and pass through them. They're the ones that survive and thrive. It's like the open, uncluttered space that Jesus teaches us to cultivate within ourselves, in the Aramaic Lord's Prayer. The trees that are full, without clear spaces, sometimes fall as a result of the storm, but they too continue to be part of the natural flow of nature. They then nurture the ground around them. In nature, there is so much contentment with what is."

We sat together with that for quite some time, letting contentment soak into our bones.

"Sam, when I come out here, I remember."

"Tell me more."

"I remember that the Source we emerged from, the Source we all *are*, allows us and everything else to be what it is. It allows us to become what we choose to become—or not."

Sam thought about that for a while. "Looking at all this allowing going on out here, reminds me that nature reflects the essence of its Source."

"Beautiful, Sam. What are you feeling in this moment?"

"Contentment," Sam quickly said, never taking his eyes off the trees.

"And it feels good? Like coming home?" I asked.

Sam smiled. "Of course! And I think I'm starting to remember why that is."

"You know, Sam, I've shared a life with an ego that is constantly living from judgment and commentary—all that like/dislike, want/don't want, should/shouldn't be happening, good/bad. It feels wonderful to go to nature and take a break from it all. It feels good to rest, to just be in the letting be, to remember."

Silence.

"That's what we are in our essence, Sam, that kind of grace."

We stood up and left the nature preserve. As we were walking to the parking lot, Sam mentioned how good it felt to be away from the world.

"This is the world," I said pointing back to the preserve, "the one before humans created theirs."

"Yeah, I know. I was talking about being away from the news."

I invited him to my house the following week to watch the very thing he wanted to get away from—the news.

"Oh joy!" Sam said. "Sounds like a great time."

I suggested that perhaps he could gain another perspective. Since feeling depressed was his primary perspective, he said he was open to a new one.

Before we drove off, I gave Sam his next remembering assignment: to practice gratitude.

11

At Home with the News: Observing the World

SAM CAME TO MY DOOR just as the nightly news was about to begin. I offered him a Sam Adams beer, and we sat down in front of the television. The news began with the usual summary of the day's stories: gun violence, women's rights being taken away, war, rising inflation, racially motivated violence, threats on LGBTQ+ rights, the increasing number of extreme weather events fueled by climate change, white supremacy in the US. There were stories about rising Christian nationalism, the political right and left pointing fingers and blaming each other, candidates vying for votes and demonizing their opponents, and then the customary feel-good story at the end. It was, all in all, a typical news broadcast.

I pressed pause. "Sam, what do you see as the common thread running through all those stories?"

Sam turned to me and said, "I don't know. All I know is I'm depressed as hell."

"Understandable. But what do you think is fueling all these stories?"

"Anger," Sam observed.

"And what fuels anger?"

"Fear," Sam quickly responded.

"Yeah, I'd say fear. The news summaries sound to me like, 'Okay, folks, here are the things we found for you to be afraid of today!'"

We watched the segments on gun violence, racially motivated violence, and the LGBTQ+ community being threatened. I pressed pause again, and Sam said, "I see the fear."

"The drama of the news creates more of what the ego is attracted to—fear. Fear justifies the ego. It gives it something to do."

"So it's a self-fulfilling thing," Sam observed.

"At the same time, Sam, we're here to be engaged with this world. It's important we know what's going on, so we can shine our light on it."

Sam looked out the window. "As a teacher, I want my students to know how the world works and what's happening in it."

"To be honest, what lens we see the news through is vital. When I watch the news, I try to look at it through the lens of the bigger spiritual picture. Fundamentally, these are all stories of souls, Sam— souls now incarnated as human beings. I see souls first, not humans. It helps me remember what this world that we live in really is. It truly is an Earth School for the soul, nothing more and nothing less. Souls come here to grow, mature, evolve through their experiences as humans. I get frustrated that this world isn't what I want it to be, and the people here are not what I want them to be, and I'm not what I want me to be. Then I try to remember that there are younger souls and older souls here, each on their own path of development. And most souls here, Sam, are younger souls. Younger as in needing to grow into maturity. It's not that they are bad. They're simply like green bananas that haven't ripened yet. They'll get there. We all will, but it takes a long time."

"If this truly is Earth School, then every soul is here because it has things to learn, to grow into. And that means I have to accept what this world really is—which will make life a whole lot easier."

"That makes sense," Sam responded. "Students at my school are all over the map when it comes to maturity. All I can do is offer what I can offer. They do the rest."

"That's what the Divine does with us," I replied. "It offers all of these experiences, and we as students at Earth School do the rest—or not. Young souls attach so strongly to the ego that they live in more fear. They live more self-referential lives as humans. They are less able to see themselves in relation to the whole. The stories we are seeing tonight are about people focusing on *their own* tribe, country, religion, race, sexual orientation, or political party. They are only with people who look and think and believe as they do. Most of us do the same. On television, we're seeing stories of younger souls who do not see their Oneness, their natural connection with all that is. The political story we heard was all about America and being an American. It was a God-bless-America story. An older soul is better able to move beyond God bless America to God bless the world."

"So, the older soul knows its true identity," Sam said.

"Yeah, I believe so. The older soul knows that its security and well being are rooted in its Source, not in any temporary labels here."

Sam nodded his head. "We see people as humans, but we need to remind ourselves that we're actually watching souls trying to live as humans."

"I've come to see that Shakespeare had it right when he said, 'All the world's a stage, and all the men and women merely players.' We souls are playing human roles in this giant play on earth. Souls are neither good nor bad. They are just acting their parts in their evolving stories."

"So what does all of that help you remember?" Sam asked.

"Well, for me, it means remembering the Oneness that is already within me. It raises that Oneness up into my awareness. I'm better able to put into perspective what people do *and why they do it.* I need to remind myself that I'm really looking at a soul here—a soul trying to be human, a soul that has its own things to grow into, just like mine. I find that helps me to back off my judgment just a bit and offer some grace to them. When I have that basic, underlying respect, I'm more able to have a respectful conversation and focus on solutions for the issue at hand, rather than focusing so much on *them.* It's still hard, but I can take steps in that direction."

"Oh my! That's tough to do!" Sam said shaking his head.

"*Super* tough," I responded, "but the difficulty serves our growth and the evolution of our souls. Everything works together as One."

"The universe is always expanding in all directions, like a balloon being stretched. I guess we're evolving like that too," Sam concluded.

"Yeah. Profound sadness stretches us to receive a deeper joy. Hopelessness allows us to know an abiding hope. That sort of thing."

We sat in silence for a bit, and then I said, "I love what Rainer Maria Rilke wrote: 'I live my life in widening circles.' As the news shows us every day, we're tribal creatures, Sam. We gravitate toward our own, so it's hard to open ourselves up to what is different. But when we do, we expand, and in its joy, our soul will let us know it is realizing its destiny. As we've talked about, that's exactly why our souls have come here—to expand, to evolve. It's their natural instinct, the natural instinct of everything!"

"Hmm, Tim. Makes sense. The universe and souls evolve in the same way—by expanding."

"I talk sometimes, Sam, with people who have really been steeped in the Church and have felt the need to leave or seek a broader, more inclusive spirituality. They tell me that the guilt that was laid on them by the Church accompanies them as they leave, as if they're doing something wrong. I want to tell them that their soul is merely doing what it came here to do—grow and evolve. Their soul is telling them that it can't breathe or live anymore in the cramped box it's been put in. It wants to take in some fresh air."

"Tim, all this reminds me that we just have to do what we have to do. Watching the news reminds me that sometimes we have to stand up for what we believe in."

"Absolutely, Sam! When we see the environment being abused—when we see women, people of color, those with another sexual orientation, the marginalized, anyone made to feel less than someone else, the Oneness is being violated. We're all a part of it.

"However, remember perspective, my friend. All the imperfections here provide the challenges our souls need. I once heard a woman speak of her near-death experience. She said that when she crossed over, she realized that we all want to change the world, but the world's purpose is to change us.

"That resonated with me and reminded me of a quote from Rumi: 'Yesterday I was clever, so I wanted to change the world. Today I am wise, so I am changing myself.'

"It's then that the light of our transformation can naturally change the world around us."

"So in practical terms, what can we do with everything we're talking about here, Tim?"

"Well, I've found it helpful to be intentional about the lens through which I watch the world. I try not to wake up and immediately turn on the news or look at a website or newspaper. If I do, I'm going to see the world through the lens of my ego and its fear. Instead, when I wake up, I first ground myself in the Oneness. We all can do that in ways that work for us. Then we engage with the world from the love and Oneness that has been raised up into our consciousness.

"How did practicing gratitude go for you, Sam?"

"It's amazing how quickly gratitude turns you around. You really do start to remember the goodness all around you. Gratitude feels so good, so right."

"Gratitude's our natural habitat. We all emerged from goodness and love, and something in our soul innately knows it's all pure gift. Gratitude is life naturally helping us greet our truth and the truth of all reality."

I could feel tears welling up as I said, "People out there look to me for help, Sam, but I grow weary of this world, and I weep for it. I see what it could be. But I know that, at any given moment, due to the current state of evolution of the souls that are here, it simply can't be different than it is. I find a strange comfort in that. Even so, I'm here to join the Universe in kicking the can of evolution down the road to remembering, if only for the tiniest fraction of an inch.

"I still get overwhelmed by the news sometimes, Sam," I said, looking down at the floor. "Sometimes, for all I've said to you in our times together, it's just a struggle for me. I struggle with being human. I struggle with my limitations. It's like a friend of mine who told me what his mentor told him: 'I know what to do. The trouble is I'm just not very good at it.'"

After a pause, Sam turned to me and put his hand on my shoulder. "I think it's time for *me* to help *you* remember something, Tim. I think people like me come to you *because* you are human, not in spite of it. You're not afraid to show your own vulnerability. You've shown it to me—at Ole's, under the stars, on the golf course, now. That's a big reason for my wanting to meet with you. Thanks for being human, Tim. Didn't you say that we're all coming to each other for safe harbor?"

"Oh, my dear Sam. Thank you. I find the same in you. And thank *you* for *choosing* to be human, Sam. That takes a lot of courage."

We sat there, looking out the window at the world our souls chose to enter.

After a few minutes, as I walked Sam out to his car, I exclaimed, "Holy crap, Sam! We've been so freakin' serious during our time together. Let's lighten up already! How about coming back and we'll watch some comedy, just to laugh together?"

Sam laughed, "Sure! I could use that."

"Awesome. Come back next week, and we'll watch whatever makes you laugh."

"I love the Pink Panther movies. I love *M*A*S*H* and *Friends.*"

"I'll have them ready to go, Sam!"

As Sam got into his car he asked me about the next remembering assignment.

"This one is for both of us, Sam. We'll send love to the people in the news."

12

At Home: Laughing

WHEN SAM KNOCKED ON THE door, I waved him in. I asked him about the remembering assignment of sending love to the people we saw in the news.

"At first I wasn't sure how to do it," Sam responded, "but then I just pictured the people I saw in the news and started saying to them, 'I love you. I send you love. You *are* love.'"

"It's simple isn't it, Sam? When I send love, I feel my own hopelessness and despair healing."

Sam smiled. "I realized this is quantum stuff we're talking about here. Everything's connected. Love is quantum."

"That's beautiful, Sam—quantum love. We may tend to think that sending love can't really make a difference, but in quantum terms, we know it can."

I already had a favorite scene cued up from *The Pink Panther Strikes Again*. Inspector Clouseau is checking himself into a hotel in Germany. Clouseau says to the hotel clerk, in his ridiculous French accent, "Have you got a rheum?"

The hotel desk clerk looks at Clouseau, "I do not know what a rheum is."

Clouseau takes out his French-German dictionary. "A *zimmer!*"

"Ah!" says the desk clerk. "A rheum!"

Clouseau says, "That is what I have been saying, you idiot!"

Clouseau notices a little dog lying on the hotel lobby floor. He asks the hotel clerk, "Does your deug bite?"

"No," the hotel clerk says.

Clouseau reaches down to pet the dog, and it growls and snaps at him. Clouseau steps back and says, "I thought you said your deug does not bite!?"

"That is not my deug!" the clerk says.

"Love that scene!" Sam said.

––––––––

We moved on to some of our favorite scenes from *M*A*S*H*. In the first, Radar walks up to Colonel Blake's desk. Before he sees Radar, Blake starts to call out, "Ra—!" Startled when he sees Radar standing there, Blake says, "Man, I don't know how you know I want to see you before *I* even know I want to see you!"

"Well, I don't like to be late, sir," Radar replies.

Next came an episode of *Friends*. Joey asks Phoebe to help him with something and Phoebe says, "Oh. I wish I could. But I don't want to."

"One of the greatest lines ever in a sitcom," I said. "Wouldn't you just love to be able to say that sometimes?

"My dad and I loved to watch comedy together. Physical comedy was our favorite. It's the contrast between expectation and reality. Nothing made us laugh more than someone tripping. Even just a good, loud sneeze would crack us up. I mean, we're all trying to look like we've got it together, and we don't. We're funny just being ourselves. I think it's because of my dad that I've always been very intentional about including humor in my life every day."

Sam shook his head. "I don't know how people can get through life being so serious."

"I don't either! I love the quote from Oscar Wilde, 'Life is too important to be taken seriously.' So true! Life is about important things—love, growing, learning."

"Yeah, I can't do any of that without laughter!" Sam declared.

I nodded. "Ethel Barrymore had it right, when she said, 'You grow up the day you have your first real laugh at yourself.' Don't you just love being around people who don't take themselves so seriously? You can just be yourself around them. They live in this place of grace and acceptance, that safe harbor that we're all looking for. There's a reason we're all looking for it. Grace, acceptance is what we all emerged from, and when we're around someone like that, it's life once again naturally helping us remember the grace we truly are."

Sam nodded. "Ha! I've known that grace from some of my friends."

"Oh Sam," I said, shaking my head, "I've known that in you. I sure as heck know that I live this life better when I'm laughing as much as possible, when I don't take all of it so seriously—especially myself."

Thinking of Inspector Clouseau and that dog in the hotel lobby, I said, "I used to do a little dog and pony show called 'The Church Is a Funny Place.' I just told stories of funny stuff that happens in churches."

"Hmm," Sam mused, "Church is not the first place that comes to mind when I think of comedy."

"Oh, it's perfect for humor, Sam! What makes something funny is often the contrast between expectation and reality. I mean here we are in church, trying to be all holy, and all this humanity breaks out. There was the time I was serving communion, and I accidentally dropped the wafer, which fell into a woman's cleavage. So, there we were, with her looking up at me and me standing there looking at her. What to do? She didn't miss a beat and said, 'I'll get it later!' We laughed about that for years!

"Then there was the time when I was in college and I interviewed for a job as church youth director. I met with the pastor in his office, and then we walked together to the youth room where the interview committee was waiting. I didn't notice the small step up into the room, and I tripped and landed on all fours. I looked up and said to the committee, 'What do you think of me so far?' (I got the job.)

"Then years later when I would visit people in memory care units, oftentimes I couldn't remember the code to get out. Funny thing was, it was always 1-2-3-4. 'Tim, your room is ready!'

"And there was the time I called God 'Bob'!"

"You called God 'Bob'?!"

"Yup. I'm officiating this baptism, and all of a sudden, I think I said 'Bob,' where I was supposed to say 'God.' While the baptism service is coming out of my mouth I'm doing a replay in my head, and it hits me. I did say Bob! I just called God 'Bob'! Then I wonder if anyone else heard it. So I'm looking around, and I see one of the family members, with her head tilted a little, looking at me like, 'Did you just call God "Bob"?' Then I started to wonder, did I baptize the baby in the name of Bob? And if I did, would it still count?"

I continued. "And my bathroom stories are legendary."

"Your what?" Sam asked.

"My bathroom stories. I once went to a pastor friend's church to lead a group discussion. Just before it was to start, I went into the bathroom. I was sitting there, and I heard two girls walk in. I thought, 'Oh, those poor girls. They went into the wrong bathroom!' Once I realized that *they* weren't the ones in the wrong room, I lifted my feet up off the floor! So there I sat, waiting them out, but they kept talking and talking and talking. Finally they left, and I ran out of there to start the group—late. And no one knew!

"And of course, there was the time I left my mic on in the bathroom, just before a wedding. I'll let you imagine it from there,"

Sam laughed so hard!

"Sam, you wanted to meet with me to learn about knowing and living from our natural Oneness with the One, everyone and everything. Laughter is one of the most fun and effective ways we can do that.

"We're One with our life Source when we're laughing. Source gives us life through laughter. Laughter lowers blood pressure and increases the production of endorphins, the body's natural painkiller. It increases the production of serotonin, dopamine, and oxytocin, so laughter reduces stress in the body and elevates our mood. It's good for the heart. My friend Joel Goodman always said, 'Laughter is internal jogging.'

"Years ago I put together my Ten Commandments of Humor. The first commandment was that Oscar Wilde quote I mentioned, 'Life is too important to be taken seriously.' We're in a much better position to be in this world, and be light for this world, after we've laughed."

"That can't all just be a coincidence," Sam responded.

"No, it isn't. I love how laughter connects people and gives us an experience of Oneness. Victor Borge, who traveled the world performing his comedy via music, said 'Laughter is the shortest distance between two people.'"

Sam sat back in his chair. "Nothing brings people together who are different from each other or don't know each other, quite like sharing a laugh."

"So true. One evening when I was in the African country of Togo, the group I was with went to an outdoor restaurant. There was live music and a dance floor. I ran out to the dance floor and made up this goofy dance I called 'the chicken dance.' I was wobbling my legs back and forth while flapping my arms like they were wings. The people around me pointed at me, laughed, and started doing the chicken dance! We were all laughing and having a good time.

"The next night we went back to the restaurant, and when we got there they were doing the chicken dance! I ran out and started dancing with them. They recognized me, and it was awesome. We couldn't communicate with each other in any other way, except by doing the chicken dance and laughing together. We didn't need another way. We were totally connected!

"When we laugh together, Sam, there's this moment where we leave our small self and meet someone else in the space of funny.

We leave our minds for just a moment and meet in this space of pure being, which is our true nature."

Sam added, "I love what Anne Lamott said, 'Laughter is carbonated holiness.'"

"That says it all, Sam!"

So it went. Two guys got together and laughed. And God laughed, and said that it was good.

13
At the Hospice Home: Moving On

AFTER A CONVERSATION ABOUT LAUGHTER, the most obvious place to go is, of course, a hospice home. Wait, what?

Actually, Sam and I first had another conversation on the phone that got into some questions about death. It took me awhile to get Sam to agree to my unusual proposal, but he eventually said he would go with me to a hospice care facility that I had often visited as a pastor. In late August, I called ahead to speak to a staff person I knew, and she confirmed that there was a room where Sam and I could meet.

I met Sam at the entrance. I asked him if he'd ever been in one of these places. He said he had, when his mother was dying—thus his hesitation. We walked into the empty room. Sam stood on one side of the bed, and I stood on the other. I told Sam I wanted us to just take in the space.

"Life gets distilled down to its essence here, Sam. I saw it over and over. Death has a way of being one of those guests Rumi spoke of in that poem you love, 'The Guest House': 'clearing you out for some new delight.' It's like all the clutter, busyness, and distractions of our lives clear out, and life distills down to what it was all along. It's all about three words: I love you. I love you, Mom. I love you, Dad. I love you, my child. I love you, love of my life. The tears and sometimes laughter are all here, even in the functionally dysfunctional families."

I looked around the room, as memories of specific people and families rolled around in my mind. "I could have told you about this space, but you've got to feel it rising up into your awareness. Feel the space. That's why I brought you here.

"Did you ever notice that, at a funeral or memorial service, people get up and talk about the love they received from the person whose picture and name are on the front of the service bulletin? In all my years, I never heard anyone speak about the house the person lived in, the car they drove, the toys they had. Someone might mention their job title or what they did for work, but even *that* is mentioned in terms of the love they showed there, the influence they had on everyone around them."

I paused. "People always go to the love they knew. I think it goes well beyond being nice or saying what's expected. Everyone talks about love so naturally at those times. I think that really says something."

"We really do know, deep down, what it's all about," Sam looked around. "I remember when my mom was in a place like this. She was in and out of consciousness for three or four days. Whenever she was conscious, we'd do the distilling you talk about." He shook his head. "She kept talking about her mom being there. Her mom had passed twenty years before. She talked to her like she was in the room. I just let her go on. I wasn't sure what to make of it."

"That's real, Sam! I've seen it happen again and again. When someone has one foot here and one foot on the other side, Love comes, in one form or another. The presence reassures them that they are on their way back to the Love they came from."

"It's amazing what can happen," I continued. "My mother-in-law was at a hospice center that had deer nearby. The staff said they knew when someone was about to pass, because the deer would come to the window. The deer knew somehow, Sam, like it was their appointed calling."

I shook my head. "The Oneness is amazing, fascinating—the Oneness of all living things."

Sam and I just stood in the silence, and I thought, "If these walls could talk . . ."

Looking at the sofa bed and chairs, Sam reflected, "It's amazing how we don't even want to talk about death. Even when we're talking about it, we're not talking about it. We say, '*If something* should happen to me.' Well, there's no 'if'—and that 'something' is dying."

"Amen, my friend! There are some people who can be direct about it all. On Ash Wednesday several years ago, I was standing at the entrance to the sanctuary, putting ashes on people's foreheads as they came in. It's supposed to be this somber thing. In walks Betty. She was a character! She just blurted out whatever was on her mind. I loved her! After I put the ashes on her forehead and said the words, 'You are but dust, and to dust you shall return,' she blurted out, 'Ain't that the truth!'"

I looked out the window at the woods behind the facility. "When I was twenty-three years old, I set off on a hike on the Gunflint Trail, north of Grand Marais, Minnesota. It was winter, and I started hiking from the road into Clearwater Lake, heading toward a beaver pond deep in the woods. It was snowing, and as I hiked it began snowing harder and harder. I remember how huge the flakes were, bigger than I had ever seen.

"I arrived at the beaver pond, got out the lunch I had packed, and hung around for a while. The snow-covered woods and the pond were absolutely beautiful. It was a time of complete and peaceful solitude. All I could hear was the occasional bird, and I swore I could hear those huge snowflakes falling on the ground.

"When I started hiking back, I noticed that the footprints I had made on my hike into the pond were already completely filled in. I stopped and thought, 'This is my life. Over time, the tracks I make on this earth will be completely covered over.'

"I've since thought about what some call the second death. That's when everyone who knew me will themselves have died. Their own lives will then be covered over by the passing of time, and there will be no one on earth who knew me. My name may turn up occasionally, if someone is interested in family history. Beyond that, it's all like a blanket of fresh snow.

"The ego struggles so much with that reality, Sam. You may be feeling your own ego's sadness and resistance now. But here is the great truth, my friend: the disappearance of the small self, the one we spend so much time obsessing over while we are here, does not matter.

"The only thing that matters is the imprints or impressions of love that we leave within everyone we walk with. Those people go on to walk in their own stories, affecting everyone and everything around them. And the story goes on for all of them and for our souls when they leave the body. In the crossing over comes the big remembering: 'Ah! I've been here before! I remember now. This is home. This is what I am. I remember now.'"

We stood on either side of the bed in silence. "It can so easily look like it all ends here, Sam, when death is actually the ultimate illusion. It's a transition that doesn't break the bonds of connection and love, either here or beyond. My friend, Echo Bodine, calls it a graduation. Those markers we see at a cemetery? I see them now as diplomas. We've completed our course on earth, and now we enter into graduate school, where learning, growth, and the journey of the soul continue. That's the journey into Love."

As I glanced over at the sofa and chairs where I saw so many families and friends sit vigil, I remembered. "Sometimes I saw people grieve for what wasn't—for what was not there in the relationship that they wanted so desperately."

Sam stared at the bed. "I know I did that with both my parents." He stood in the silence for a while, as he was remembering. "Hmm, a dysfunctionally functional family? Maybe it's true what you say, Tim, about all of the people in my life. We weren't perfect, but we were perfect for each other. I'm starting to see the truth of that. I wouldn't be who and what I am without them. Part of me still wishes it had been different, of course, but I guess it all served a purpose. It's like you say, we're all here working on something together. They had their paths, and I had mine."

As we walked to the door, I turned around, looked back at the bed, and remembered the three word conversations I heard so often. Those conversations revealed what their time together had been about all along.

"I love you, Sam!"

"I love you too, Tim."

As we left the hospice home, Sam told me that he felt the need to go out to the woods and the open space that we had shared. He needed to breathe. He needed to consider the mark he wanted to leave here in the people he had accompanied.

As I watched Sam walk away, I thought about our helping each other to remember our Oneness with God and with all that is. "Be well my friend, on your journey to where you've always been."

Acknowledgments

A MAJOR REASON I KNEW I was supposed to write this book is the village of angels I had surrounding me and making it possible. I offer my heartfelt thanks.

To my wife, Doree, whose constant love, support, and wisdom have made not only this book possible but also my life.

To our daughters, Sonja and Sarah, sons-in-law, Jonathan and Luke, and our grandchildren, Soren and Olivia: You help me remember the melody of love in the music of life.

To my soul sister, Sue Hein, for endless hours of processing, being honest with me, and helping me find my writing voice.

To Mark Pitzele, Sue Hein, and Mackenzie Rasmus for helping me find the conversational format of this book.

To my dear friend, Melissa Anderson, for her wisdom, tireless editing, and encouragement.

To artist, illustrator, and friend, Bill Beaupre, who always saw a way to make visual what was in my mind and heart.

To Echo Bodine, who guided me to remember the Love from which we have all come, who believes in me, and has given me every opportunity to share my truth with the world: I'm deeply grateful for your kind words in your lovely foreword.

To my Wednesday discussion group: Diane, Terrie, Sue, Joanne, Dan, Jean, Kim, Joanne, Caren, Craig, Jerry, Joyce, Bill, and Jill. Our sense of community has helped me remember the Oneness we share. You are love!

To the readers of my column I Remember Now on echobodine.com: Thank you for your encouragement and support.

To my parents and sister, Grant, Eva, and Mary, and to the wonderful people in the congregations I served: You provided me a foundation of love from which to begin my exploration.

To Jen Weigel for introducing me to the wonderful people at Pen & Publish, and for helping me spread the word.

Finally to the One(ness), which clearly let me know there was a book in me that would not let me go.

Made in the USA
Monee, IL
20 December 2024

74694530R00079